The Foundations Of A Successful Property Investor

Harvey Raybould

Copyright © 2020 Harvey Raybould

All rights reserved.

ISBN-13: 978-1-9163800-0-4

Table of Contents

Introduction ·· vii

About The Author ··· xi

Chapter 1 Your Success, Your Way – I Am Who I Am ···················· 1

Chapter 2 Success Starts with Taking a Leap of Faith ····················· 6

Chapter 3 The Mindset and Success Principles of

Professional Property Investors ································ 16

Chapter 4 Finding and Protecting Your Creative Time ·················· 23

Chapter 5 The Importance of Consistency,

Routines and Repetition ·· 28

Chapter 6 Do Less to Achieve More ····································· 32

Chapter 7 The Liberation of Personal Growth ·························· 39

Chapter 8 Do You Need To Learn About Yourself? ···················· 50

Chapter 9 The One-Hour Principle For Working On Yourself ·········· 63

Chapter 10	Why Knowing The Person You Are Is Key To Your Success	68
Chapter 11	Your Fascination Language – Get Past The First Nine Seconds	76
Chapter 12	How To Set Goals That Will Inspire You	82
Chapter 13	The Importance Of Knowing What You Need And What You Want	91
Chapter 14	Pulling It All Together And What To Do Next	101
	Conclusion	113

Introduction

> "The biggest risk is not taking any risk ... In a world that's changing really quickly, the only strategy that is guaranteed to fail is not taking risks."
> — MARK ZUCKERBERG

Firstly, thank you very much for taking the time to read this book. It shows that you are serious about your property investment success and becoming the best investor that you can be, and the obvious rewards this will bring you.

The contents of this book have been gleaned from my own personal experiences and journey in business and property over the last twenty years, It is packed full of techniques, tips and exercises that will enable you to take your property investment onto the next level, building more freedom and earning the sums of money you truly desire.

This is my first endeavour at being an author, and I would never have believed that I would have dreamed of writing a book, let alone completing one and getting it published. To be frank, English wasn't my best subject at school.

In my second year, we had twenty in my class. In all subjects I was in the top three pupils, except for English where I came eighteenth in the final exam. My form teacher, who taught us English, was angry with me and just couldn't understand it, I even failed my English 'O' Level first time round. I was always more Maths orientated, and enjoyed those types of subjects to a much greater extent.

So, if you are thinking of writing a book and sharing your knowledge, but are being put off by your literary skills, don't worry, just go for it. As long as you are passionate about your subject and about helping other people, and carry out all that needs to be done with consistent effort, you can definitely pull it off. I am living proof.

How This Book Will Help You

This book, will teach you how to prepare yourself to become a successful property investor. Your mindset is crucial to your success, and it is essential that we start here.

We'll be discussing the mindset principles of what it takes to be successful in the property business and in your life.

The Foundations Workbook

This is a doing book - the emphasis is very much on practical things that you can do regularly, that will make a real difference to you and your property business. To put these principles to work requires no previous expertise or experience, but does require some consistent effort.

I have created a special Foundations Workbook for you, to guide you through the whole process in an easy to follow way. There are clear action steps at every stage that will challenge you at times, but with some perseverance and dedication, are more than achievable for anyone with a true desire to win. There are even examples in the Workbook to guide you. It is a must-have as it will make your journey a whole lot easier.

Download your FREE Foundations Workbook and other bonus documents here:

http://www.freedomviaproperty.com/downloads

INTRODUCTION

Don't just read it and set it aside

I would never have been able to write this book or lived in the places I have, met so many great people or made lifelong friendships without adopting the principles that are within this book.

It might not be your goal to live in another country, as I have done, but whatever your "why" is, you can achieve anything you want with consistent effort. Consistency is in my opinion the number one way to get where you want to go, in the shortest amount of time, without becoming overwhelmed and eventually giving up. By consistency, I mean small efforts made regularly. This is the basis for the one-hour principle described later in this book.

But, and here's the "but": to get the most out of this book, you can't just read it and set it aside. You have to do the exercises and use the techniques. This book can transform you and help you to achieve a more satisfying and successful life. But only if you put the work in!

A football coach trains and advises their team but ultimately must trust the players to go out and deliver on the field. So think of me as your "Property Success" coach. My job is to offer you proven techniques and exercises. But you are the one who has to go out on the football pitch of your own life.

So let's get started

I want to wish you good luck, but I really don't think you will need it. Your success and freedom are within your control and by starting to read this book, you have already demonstrated the will to achieve everything you truly desire. Do the work and you will win. It really is that simple. So, I hope that you enjoy the journey and please drop me an email to let me know how you've got on.

All the best
Harvey Raybould
harvey@freedomviaproperty.com

About The Author

The Number One Question

I guess the number one question that needs answering is why am I qualified to write a book of this nature? Well, I have been running successful businesses for over twenty years, in both IT and property.

From a very early age, I had the entrepreneurial bug, and was constantly looking for the next thing I could make money from. I think I was about fourteen or fifteen when I had my first business, and went through dozens of business ideas before I started to gain some success in my mid to late twenties.

I have the never-give-up mentality and failure was never something that put me off. Risk-taking I guess is in my blood, and the willingness to sacrifice in the short-term for longer- term gains is what I have done and continue to do from time to time.

However, about twelve years ago, I made a lifestyle choice to be able to live anywhere I wanted to, but which would also allow me to be able to run my businesses efficiently from wherever I am. I love travelling and often get itchy feet, and don't like to be tied down to one place for too long.

So, I made the jump, started putting the plans into action and have been very fortunate to have lived in some amazing places over the last ten years or so. Barcelona, Marbella, Phuket, Bangkok are just some of the places I have lived, as well as travelling to many different countries for extended periods while still being able to work.

THE FOUNDATIONS OF A SUCCESSFUL PROPERTY INVESTOR

On 23 December 2014, I got diagnosed with cancer. I was in Bangkok at the time and was in a huge dilemma about what to do. To be honest, it came as a massive shock, as I'd never really been ill all my life and just hearing that C word is enough to scare you to death.

I could have had the operation in Bangkok, as some of their hospitals are absolutely world-class, but decided to come back to the UK. However it was Christmas and I didn't want to spoil my family's festive time, so I didn't tell them straight away. I was supposed to stay out there for another couple of months, but I rearranged my flight and flew back unannounced on the 28th.

Telling my family wasn't easy, it came as a huge blow to them as well. Strangely, for me, anyway, I think it was harder on my family than it was on me. I think that was solely to do with my mindset. I never really tried to think or worry about it. I never believed I was ill, and I definitely never thought something like that would beat me.

I had been relatively successful in my life up to that point, but looking back now I think I had been drawn into a comfort zone, I didn't have any money worries, no debt apart from the mortgages on my properties, travelling seven months or so of the year, and having a good comfortable life.

But finding out I had cancer made me realise I didn't want a comfortable life. There were things I wanted to achieve and experience and I needed to get off my arse if these were going to happen.

On 25 March 2015, I had an operation to remove a tennis ball sized tumour, but in the end, they had to remove my right kidney as well. I couldn't have asked for better care in the NHS hospital I stayed in, and cannot thank the nurses and doctors enough for all the help and care they gave me.

However, I was only in there for two nights, I hardly needed any morphine, and two hours after the operation, I was reading *Influence* by Robert Cialdini (the classic book on persuasion, which explains the psychology of why peo-

ABOUT THE AUTHOR

ple say "yes"). All the while answering emails on my phone. The nurses were quite amazed at my recovery speed, and when the consultant saw me on the third morning he agreed I could be discharged. I was thankful to be going home, not because of the food or bad care but if you have ever tried to sleep properly in a hospital it is impossible, with all the noise and activity going on. So I was really looking forward to a great night's sleep.

So, what is the moral of this story? I'm not physically stronger or fitter than most people, but I do believe I have a fitter and stronger mental attitude than a lot of people I know.

In 2015 despite having my operation and a few months of recovery, I was able to buy and sell over £1million worth of property and started expanding my team. I'd set out new visions and goals for my property business, increased turnover and profitability, read thirty plus books, all whilst spending four months outside of the UK, in SE Asia.

I can promise you that I am not telling you this to brag, as I really think I should have actually achieved more in that time, but just to let you know that despite anything that life throws at you, you can, with the right attitude, accomplish anything you truly desire. And just so you know, you don't have to be born with the right attitude, it is definitely something you can learn if you take action and apply yourself.

CHAPTER 1
Your Success, Your Way – I Am Who I Am

> "Be yourself: everyone else is already taken."
> — Oscar Wilde

Although I am going to share a lot of examples and stories in this book, it is imperative that you create "Your Success, Your Way". Your property investment business needs to reflect your personality, your values, your ambitions. This is what will make it unique, and what will make it stand out from the crowd.

Don't blindly copy what everyone else is doing or suggesting. Do what makes you feel comfortable.

For those of you who have come into the property business from a non-business background (and that is generally most people, so don't worry), creating "Your Success, Your Way" might be a strange concept but this book will help you every step of the way. If you complete all the exercises, by the end, you will have the basis to create a property investment business that is talking in your unique VOICE, one that can grow into your VISION and one that is built on your GUIDING PRINCIPLES.

The key to standing out is looking inward.

Entrepreneurs that intend to define their own style and brand will often use one of the following approaches.

1. Make it up as they go
2. Follow someone else's lead

Property Investors That Make It Up As They Go

What comes to mind when you think of making a critical decision as you go? To me, I imagine driving at seventy miles an hour on the motorway with a windscreen cover on. Very scary indeed. By deciding to carry on with a property investment business before pinning down your guiding principles, values, and ideals, you are placing yourself in a disadvantaged position. That will cause you to become reactive rather than proactive. You'll always be trying to solve challenges instead of achieving goals and meeting targets.

Additionally, day to day decisions become almost impossible to make as your team lack guidelines on how to operate. Such a property investment business will have a hard time trying to gain traction in this rapidly evolving market, due to the random nature of their approach. As you may well be aware, the property business is largely based on mutual trust. Part of this trust is earned through having a clear track record of consistency.

When an entrepreneur is making up guidelines and approaches as they go, consistency is broken and so is base trust. People are unsure of your principles and guidelines and therefore feel as though they cannot rely on you and your team to give sustained positive returns.

This lack of consistency also affects your team who, at the slightest inconvenience or shift in trend, have to go back to the drawing board and try to re-think their next course of action.

Property Investors That Follow Someone Else's Lead

The property business demands that you are able to acquire new information and learn. One source of this information and learning is a mentor – which is absolutely okay. However, this is not to mean that you are to clone the solution offered by the mentor. Remember, businesses and personalities are not the same and whatever works for your mentor may not always work for you. It can lead you to wonder why their great tactics are not working in your favour.

Additionally, reliance on a mentor's guidance is not only detrimental for you in the short-run where you are constantly chasing the ideals set by the mentor, but also in the long-run where you have to refer back to the mentor for every new challenge or for further guidance if tactics don't work. This denies you a prime opportunity to gain confidence in your decision-making skills and also a chance to learn from your mistakes which are important foundations of successful entrepreneurs.

With that being said, it is true that mentors offer invaluable input. However, you should use this input to help you build *your* strategic plan, not to become a clone of theirs.

Success Your Way With A Strategic Plan

The premise is that every successful entrepreneur has a unique, standout style that shapes their approach. Successful entrepreneurs lay down guiding principles that permeate all their decisions to achieve their goals.

These principles are dictated by both internal and external factors that are unique to every entrepreneur. Therefore, as you seek inspiration from the people you admire, use their models and approaches as a learning tool to develop your unique ideas rather than replicating theirs. Aim at getting into your own box instead of someone else's.

Do Something Differently
Do not allow yourself to get stuck trying to build upon what others have done. Instead, model your own life so that it harnesses your key strengths while also leveraging your passion. You can achieve this by first identifying what you can do differently from any other person. If ever there were shortcuts to success, then doing something different rather than better would be the safest shortcut. In the words of Sally Hogshead, former advertising executive and best-selling author:

"Better isn't better; different is better."

By the end of this book, I would like you to embrace the belief that there is no right or wrong way to be an entrepreneur – there is only your way. Forget the noise about how it has always been done and so that is how you must do it. Forget also the notion that you should strive to do better than your competitors. Start thinking differently, not better.

Summary
So, what did we learn? Well, first and foremost, it is important to have a strategic plan. Additionally, a model/strategy is one that speaks your unique voice, grows into your vision and is based on your unique personality and guiding principles.

Whereas mentors might offer great input to this end, they are not the final say in what you do. Grow into your own, identify what you can do differently and then leverage your passion and strengths to materialise your strategic plan. In all, the foundation for a successful property investor is doing things your way guided by a strategic plan.

CHAPTER 1

Action Points

Start to think about what you can do differently, what is your opportunity to do something different, how is your process different? Think differently, not better!!! Once you have some ideas, write them down in your Workbook that you can get here.

Download your FREE Foundations Workbook and other bonus documents here:

http://www.freedomviaproperty.com/downloads

CHAPTER 2
Success Starts with Taking a Leap of Faith

> "Success is stumbling from failure to
> failure, with no loss of enthusiasm."
> — SIR WINSTON CHURCHILL

Although it sounds ironic, it is true that the most consistent thing in life is change. However, I have not met a single person who can proclaim that they are not scared of change in one way or the other. We are inherently uncomfortable with the anxiety, turmoil and extreme probabilities presented by change.

With that being said, we also desire for better things in life as dictated by the Maslow's hierarchy of needs theory (see diagram below): we are always in constant search for higher level needs. Meeting one need is not an end in itself but rather the starting point for the push towards higher needs. However, it is not possible to meet our higher level needs while still in a status quo. If we are to move forward, the rubber must hit the road and things must change.

CHAPTER 2

Maslow's hierarchy of needs

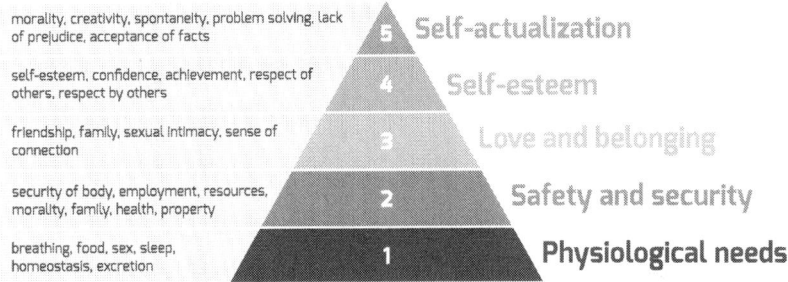

As an entrepreneur who has had to risk everything several times, this is easier said than done. The reality is that most of us wait until we are certain of success before starting on new ventures. We are always afraid of failing, afraid that we will not meet the amazing result that we envision and therefore choose to abandon the ventures entirely.

I am not saying that fear is a flaw. On the contrary, it is a part of us. As a matter of fact, it keeps us safe. If it were not for fear we would all be running on tightropes across Tower Bridge and paragliding down the Himalayas.

The sad part is that the same fear that keeps us away from doing potentially fatal things also keeps us from taking action on ventures that could be of monumental benefit to us. This is because we become so invested in the consequences of failure and thereby form a mental picture to the effect that failure would be the end of the world.

In essence, we desire to accomplish greater things in life, but we also realise that we need to take action to get from where we are to where we want to be. But the fear of the unknown and fear of failure stops us from taking action. At this point of crisis, we need to take a leap of faith. I am not talking about closing our eyes and just letting what will be, be, but rather changing our view on the process of action and accomplishment.

Here is a true story from my own life that demonstrates the power of taking a leap of faith. When I was much younger I had a good job at a bank in the City of London. But I wasn't happy at this job. I hated commuting to the city every day but it was more than that. I had the entrepreneurial bug.

My father was planning to retire from running his own business. He told my brother and I that he wanted us to take over the business. We both agreed and I told my boss at the bank that I wanted to quit. He talked me out of quitting temporarily by offering me more money.

I spent another 6 months at the bank but I really couldn't stand it anymore and dreamed of running my father's business with my brother. So I quit for good. The problem was that my brother had decided to go and do something else and my father had changed his mind about retirement! So I had nothing.

But this did not deter me. I created a number of leaflets offering a local gardening service to homeowners. This worked really well and in no time I had a number of regular customers. I moved on from this and got involved in more successful ventures and I have never worked for anyone else since.

Accomplishments As Starting Points

As businessman and bestselling author Harvey Mackay, notes: "A great accomplishment shouldn't be the end of the road, just the starting point for the next leap forward."- *Pushing the Envelope. All the Way to the Top*

When we think of success, we often analogise it into a utopia where we roll off into the sunset to live happily ever after. We therefore pile all our hopes on one particular goal with the mindset that on accomplishing this, it will mark the "eureka" moment in our lives.

Accomplishing the set goal brings great joy but this joy does not last. After some weeks or months, we realise that we are stagnating with no zeal or vision to do more which breeds disappointment. We fail to realise that goals are not an end in themselves but rather a foundation on which we should build more success.

If you look at it critically, goals such as losing weight, making money etc., are always a prerequisite to achieving higher goals. You may want to make more money so as to finally take your spouse on that long-delayed honeymoon or want to lose weight so that you can have a family or join a community sports team or even the army.

The overriding idea is that as humans we are ever hungry for more, and therefore accomplishments, however grand, cannot give us eternal satisfaction. Even after achieving otherwise monumental goals, we will still want more. Therefore, the more appropriate view is to take goals and accomplishments as a new, advantaged foundation upon which you can attain more success – a milestone. When we think of goals and accomplishments as just a milestone in a grand journey and not a make or break stab at eternal happiness, we become less fearful of taking that crucial leap of faith.

Being Comfortable With The Uncomfortable
Life starts at the end of your comfort zone.

Well, it is true that you cannot expect the same route you use every day to take you to a different destination. If you want a different destination, you must be willing to try out a new route. You need to take the risk. Taking risks might sound like something out of our daily norms but we are constantly taking risks – every day.

Going into the office in the morning not knowing what eventualities will arise, picking up the phone, approaching a client, making a sale or purchase.

We are constantly putting ourselves out there and leaving ourselves vulnerable to eventualities and rejection – but we still undertake these daily activities without a second thought or a shred of doubt.

Why? Because we are accustomed to them – we do them every day, whether we fail or succeed, we still push on. Failure doesn't kill us or decapitate us. `Success in these activities does not mean that we abandon work and celebrate – we keep moving. Therefore, you already have one foot in the water, you already take risks, but now it's time to bump it up a notch. Knowing that you can handle everyday risks, win or lose, and still move on builds your confidence to take on larger risks like venturing into a new market or category. With this attitude, we are no longer scared of failure.

As a matter of fact, we embrace it – we not only allow ourselves to fail but we go out there and fall flat on our faces. We know it is not the end of anything but rather a learning opportunity. The lessons learnt from failure anchor your feet while treading in future opportunities.

I have lived by these principles with my property investment business. There have been a number of times that I have had to take risks and move on from failures. As time went on I took larger risks for larger rewards and my confidence grew all of the time. I learned from my mistakes with every disappointment, and continued to push forward even when things didn't go to plan. I took risks by entering new property investment markets and all of this has got me to where I am today. You need to do the same.

There are risks with all forms of property investment. You can do a lot to mitigate risk but you can never eliminate it completely. Due diligence is the key to mitigating risk. You must know your numbers and do as much research as possible. There is no such thing as too much research. If you have to invest in an area that you are not familiar with then visit the area and find out as much as you can about it. Don't just take someone else's word for it that an area has a high private rental yield or that the property prices are below market value. In the example I gave you above I trusted in someone else's opinion and it really cost me.

You might not make a loss on a project but there may be situations where things didn't turn out as you expected. Here is a very recent example from my own business. I will appraise properties using my trusted formula and this tells me what the perceived value is likely to be at the end of the project. In the UK right now we are preparing to leave the European Union and we have called this Brexit. The surveyors and banks are now very jittery about Brexit and as a result they are down valuing a lot of properties. So Brexit and down valuing is now affecting my appraisals of properties.

This is not really a failure. I will still make good money from my current investments but not as much as I had expected. It is still a good investment but not as good as I had planned it to be. I have no control over Brexit but I should have been in touch with how surveyors and banks were feeling about it.

You need to understand that when you are starting out with property investment your risk is usually fairly low but as you progress the risks get higher because you will want to take on larger projects. Some property investors start by purchasing a small flat and then will move on to larger property purchases. There is more money at stake so the risk increases.

Here is an example of a failure that I experienced. Many years ago, before I really knew what I was doing 100%, I purchased some properties in the North West of England. One of these properties did not provide the level of returns that I had been promised it would. I purchased the property through a sourcing company and made the mistake of believing all of their numbers without doing comprehensive due diligence myself. I believed that I was buying the property at a low price and that I would achieve the monthly rental income that the company said I would.

So I went ahead and purchased the property. My first shock was receiving a bill for white goods and flooring and carpets. As this was a brand new development, I had assumed that there would have been carpeting. Once finished, I placed the property on the rental market and despite a number of viewings there were no takers. It actually took 6 months to find a tenant and I had to reduce the monthly rent by £100 less than the sourcing company had promised.

I still own this property today and it has been rented consistently with a few changes of tenant since. I am just seeing a profit now, but the main thing is that this disappointing experience did not put me off and I pushed forward with property investment. What it taught me is that buying property outside of the area that I knew was not a good idea. Also the location of a property is vital as is the proper due diligence. Since then I developed a system where I check 35 comparables before I buy a property. I also conduct comprehensive appraisals on everything before an offer is made. Property investment is risky enough and you want your risks to be calculated ones.

Looking at the entrepreneurial journey of the late Steve Jobs sparks many relatable lessons on what taking a leap of faith actually means. At a time when he was facing stiff competition from Microsoft and even harsher wrangles within his company, he remained adamant on his core belief of redefining mobile computing.

Then came the biggest blow – being fired from his own company. But when he finally came back, he was even more determined – immediately cutting down their products from sixty to just a handful which was a big risk.

Having more products would have ensured that Apple maintained a safety net against under-performing products, but Jobs had a higher vision than breaking even and being profitable. He believed he could change the world, and change the world he did. He once candidly noted that being fired from Apple replaced the heaviness of being successful with the lightness of being a beginner again which reinvigorated his focus and fuelled his hunger to take bigger risks.

It is not okay to just be okay. Real progress will not come from having a steady income flow from a niche. On the contrary, it will come from shaping the unknown and moving to the areas where you feel most uncomfortable, uncertain and even unsure of yourself. Conquering this area is your true test of FAITH and proof of your progress and success.

Faith, not in the context of religious belief but rather the firm belief that you can achieve success regardless of the cost, energy, sacrifice or time. In this context, faith is the foundation block that allows, compels and empowers dreamers to take risks and to chase their dreams.

It is a subtle trust and a feeling of confidence that you will be victorious no matter what. People who simply conclude that entrepreneurship is not for them lack this strong inherent belief.

Faith is the substance of things hoped for, the evidence of things not seen.

All the top business players that I know have one thing in common and that is faith. They all have a deep excitement, a power and the ability to exert extreme levels of focus and energy to see their objectives through. Their hope and firm belief is that, sooner or later, something will have to give, which gives them immense stimulation and confidence to take on even the biggest risks.

To break this down, envision the life of a 2-year-old or a toddler learning to walk. We know that the toddler desires to walk. From its subconscious, the toddler keeps trying to walk, falls down repeatedly but at no point does the toddler think that maybe walking was not meant for him. Even after learning how to walk, the toddler now starts trying to jump, run, ride the bike etc.

The same applies to the otherwise mischievous and hyperactive two-year-olds who always want to do everything, are defiant, resilient and will break rules despite knowing that they might be punished. As adults, we lose this enviable spirit of the toddler and the two-year-old. By putting ourselves out there, we are bound to lose from time to time. But tenacity and perseverance backed by a hindsight-based perspective is the key to making progress in life and in business. Having that perspective so that we do not repeat the same mistakes allows us to achieve the success we desire.

Remember that taking risks is not a one-off experience, it ought to be part of your life. It might take you several tries to attain some level of success but as we have established, even failure is a learning success. However, even after achieving success, view it as a milestone; as a new foundation to plan for more success.

Getting caught up in minor success is more dangerous than dealing with a defeat. A tenacious person does not get comfortable with current success, they are constantly pushing to new heights. They know that they have done the best within their abilities but need to do more for even greater success.

Summary

It is easy to shy away from opportunities because of fear and subsequently stagnate in the same position. However, we cannot realise our true potential in our comfort zones. True success and progress come from conquering opportunities and ideas with which we are unfamiliar; even those that might create great anxiety. It is at this point we need to take a leap of faith.

A faith that our best efforts and unwavering commitment will eventually yield success. This is the underlying characteristic of great entrepreneurs. They have a deep conviction, an excitement and a deep hunger to challenge new frontiers without fear of failure. They understand that failure is a learning opportunity and a building block for future success.

By viewing accomplishments and failures as nothing more than milestones in a grand journey, you can also overcome this fear of failure. Adopt the tenacity and determination of a toddler learning to walk and you will be unstoppable both in business and life.

Action Points

A Wayne Gretzky quote was constantly reiterated by Steve Jobs "I skate to where the puck is going and not to where it has been". To build an outstanding property investment business, you have to take the risk of venturing into new markets with the greatest potential.

Take stock of the trends in property investing and extrapolate where the market is heading. Then plan and act now to capitalise on the opportunity before the market responds. Make that leap of faith and be the first to explore that new opportunity you have discovered. If it doesn't work out, move on to the next opportunity and give it your all. Eventually, with faith and determination, something will have to give.

CHAPTER 3

The Mindset and Success Principles of Professional Property Investors

> "Many of life's failures are people who did not realise how close they were to success when they gave up."
> — THOMAS EDISON

As you are no doubt already investing in property if you are reading this book, or at least well on your way to thinking about it, I don't want to go into too much detail on this subject. You have probably read or heard a lot about it in the past, but I would just like this chapter to act as a refresher for you.

From the outset, having the right mindset is extremely important in anything you do, especially when it involves investing money and running a business. There are going to be times when it is tough, when you get a knock back or when things are just not moving as fast as you would like. But having that clear end goal and belief is what is going to get you through all the dark moments.

Research done by Barbara Fredrickson, a psychology professor, shows that people who are accustomed to having a positive mindset have a higher tendency to absorb new information, think rationally and thereby become better decision makers. Additionally, having the right mindset boosts your energy levels and your zeal to perform. You will attest to the fact that when you have a properly laid out and planned task, you are more inclined to perform it now than wish it away for later.

If you are not new to entrepreneurship, you appreciate that it is unlikely that you will make it big with your first venture or idea. You initially have to stumble and learn from your mistakes. During this phase, having a positive mindset that is laser-focused on the prize helps you to pick yourself up and not to give up – and trust me there are times you feel like calling it quits.

Having the right mindset does not just impact you. Positivity is infectious and if you, as the owner and leader, adopt a positive mindset, it will resonate across the business from the employees and even to your clients. This will create a very conducive environment for success.

The good thing is, it takes very minor acts to nurture a positive mindset yet the benefits are so profound. Form a culture where the following activities are promoted.

- Taking breaks off work with colleagues
- Being grateful to your team members
- Allowing team members to have their space and time
- Promoting personal goals of your team members
- Encouraging nice comments and appreciation among colleagues
- Addressing challenges professionally
- Allowing some compromise – after all, we are humans

However, it is important to remember that having the right mindset is just a foundation, you have to build on that firm foundation with positive actions.

Now that we have the basis for the positive mindset required to build and shape our businesses, let's go right back to the beginning. Think about, why you are investing in property. What do you want this investment to do for you? What is your end goal; your reason why?

THE FOUNDATIONS OF A SUCCESSFUL PROPERTY INVESTOR

In order to get into the right frame of mind for property investment, you'll need to have a concrete answer to all of these questions. You might be investing in property because you want to retire early. Perhaps you want to supplement your pension, or maybe you want to increase your income to enjoy a more lavish lifestyle.

It's possible that you're investing because you want financial freedom or security. Perhaps you want to give up your day job and move into property investment on a full-time basis. You could even be investing as a profitable hobby. Either way, the sooner you understand exactly why you're in this industry, the more you can align your goals and targets with your own mindset.

THIS IS EXTREMELY IMPORTANT: You must, must, must write down your clearly defined "Why". You need to have it somewhere visible in your workspace, so that you can read it every day, for motivation and help in getting through the bad times.

Speaking of targets – it's crucial to set realistic, achievable targets when you're investing in property or running any business. Otherwise, how else will you be able to gauge whether an investment was a success or not? Or if your business is on the right track?

There are a multitude of ways in which you can measure your achievements. Perhaps there's an ideal total that you want your bank account to hit. Maybe your target is to build a portfolio that will generate a certain amount of income every month – say, £5,000, or £10,000. Maybe you measure success by measuring rental yield. For example, you might class anything above 7% yield as a successful investment. Perhaps your definition of success is being able to retire five years early, or take that dream holiday you've always wanted.

Without these targets or ambitions, property investment becomes aimless. And without something to aim for, it becomes easier to get complacent and consider giving up.

I will be discussing goals, targets and Key Performance Indicators (KPIs) in much more detail later in this book, so at this stage I've mentioned it just to encourage you to get your thoughts going. Your sub-conscious brain is a wonderful thing, and if you put thoughts into it on a regular basis, it will work tirelessly for you, without you knowing, and come up with the answers you need.

Success Principles

In order to provide a little inspiration if you are just setting out on your property investment journey or whether you often face times when things aren't easy, I'd like to talk a little more about success principles, and how they affect our investments. Here are some of my favourite success principles, applied to the world of property:

You Don't Have To Reinvent The Wheel

Actually, you're not reinventing anything at all when it comes to property investment. You're simply taking something that already exists and adding value to it – it's really that easy.

With so much complex jargon and financial lingo to contend with, it can be easy to get swept up and make property investment more complicated than it needs to be – don't fall into the trap. You're not doing anything pioneering or world-changing, so try not to put too much pressure on yourself.

Failure Is Imminent

This success principle initially sounds discouraging – it basically says we're all set up to fail at some point. But it's how we deal with that failure which dictates whether we'll succeed or not. It was Winston Churchill who famously said, "Success is stumbling from failure to failure, with no loss of enthusiasm."

Property markets are volatile – you're not going to generate huge profit every single time you make a new investment. But if you can pick yourself up, dust yourself off and learn from your mistakes, you'll be in a better position to succeed than anyone who has never failed.

Persistence Wins Out

Don't give up. You might have a discouraging string of poor investments which didn't work out as you'd hoped. As long as they're still generating an income, and as long as you can still afford a deposit for a new property, my strong opinion is that you should always persist.

Here's a little anecdote. Back in the 1990s, Steve Jobs presided over the production of a little gadget called the Apple Newton. It was essentially a very primitive version of the tablet computers we know today, but without the technology of the digital age, it was widely disparaged. It had a poor battery life, the screen was hard to read, and the so-called 'handwriting recognition' tool, which was pioneering at the time, was so poor it was mocked outright on an episode of *The Simpsons*.

But did Steve Jobs give up? No – in fact, the Apple Newton inspired many aspects of future operating systems for Apple. If Jobs had given up after the failure of his Newton, we might not have innovations like smartphones or mainstream tablet devices today.

Positivity Leads To Productivity

You'll never be fully productive unless you're positive about it. You can't fully say that you've put your heart and soul into a project if you're feeling negative about it! It's important to remember that happiness is a key element of success. If you're not happy, can you really say you're successful? If you're feeling negative about your business, do something positive to change your mindset.

There's No Progress Without Action

This is a personal favourite of mine. Many people who approach me about property investment often find an excuse not to get involved with it straight away. "I'm planning on investing in property next year, once I have the lay of the land," they say. Or, "I'm still researching just now – I'll invest when the time is right." Here's a quick newsflash: there's never a 'right' time to invest in property – it's the right time all the time!

As this success principle states, you'll never make any progress unless you take some action – so think positive, be determined, and take the plunge.

So I hope this chapter has acted as a nice refresher for you, and got you thinking again about "YOUR WHY". Property investment is a wonderful industry, better than any I have been involved in before, as the amount of people out there willing to help is phenomenal.

I would strongly advise that you go to regular property networking meetings, join relevant Facebook groups and get involved in the communities that are out there. These have been absolutely invaluable to my development.

Summary

I purposed this chapter to be a refresher on WHY you are in property investment or otherwise why you are planning to join. This is because, we all have varying reasons for investing in property; from financial security, hobby, freedom etc. Having a clear understanding and then constantly reminding yourself on WHY you made the plunge into property investment sets your mindset right even when times become rough – it is not always rosy.

This is also important in aligning your targets, strategy and plans which collectively provide a realistic roadmap towards accomplishing the WHY. In addition to having a clear roadmap, you also need to have success guiding principles that ground you in both hard and smooth times. As an industry, property investment is well developed and there is little to no pioneering and world-changing that is needed. Therefore, quit putting too much pressure on yourself particularly on the complex jargon and financial lingo.

Focus on adding value to available systems and processes and you are good to go. Secondly, failure, particularly in the volatile property investment industry, is part of the success story for both starters and the gurus. Therefore learn to be persistent even when markets are against you, hang in there and refuse to quit.

Additionally, even in tough days – trust me they will be there, hold your head high and remain positive. Make an effort to remain positive and success will be yours. If you are not yet in property investment, the time to get started is right away. I meet people who give all manner of excuses but you will not make progress with just intentions – take the plunge and act right away.

Action Points

If you do not know where you are going, every route will lead you there. Do you still remember WHY you started in property investment? Is the passion and vision still alive? You need to reinstate the reason why you are in property investment or planning to join.

After answering the WHY, evaluate whether your plan, strategy and targets align to the WHY. If not, make the necessary changes without placing too much pressure on yourself. Stop fearing failure, it is part of the process and in its place, use a positive mindset to persistently work at your WHY until you know exactly what it is.

CHAPTER 4
Finding and Protecting Your Creative Time

> "You will never find the time for anything.
> If you want time, you must make it."
> — Charles Burton

I wake up between 4am and 5am every morning, and after doing my "Miracle Morning" routine, around 6am, is my "creative time". This is my sweet spot, and if you don't know it already you need to be able to find yours.

In his book *The Miracle Morning*, Hal Elrod explains that to become successful, you have to dedicate time each day to personal development. This is your most creative time and also the time when your brain and body is at peak performance. This time differs across people but if you are a morning person, Hal recommends a six-step morning routine to create and shape this time.

I personally draw a lot of inspiration from Hal Elrod. After being declared dead for six minutes from a car crash, he recovered and moved on to develop this morning routine that has had a very positive influence on my life. During my creative time I work on my higher-level strategies, write, read and come up with ideas. It is when I am at my best creatively.

I like early mornings because generally, no one else is around. I can't be disturbed, phones aren't going. I am disciplined to not look at my emails until at least 8 am, often later. I limit my social media in the morning to just 15 minutes so this doesn't distract me, and I concentrate on just one thing at a time.

You may think that since it is my most creative and productive time, I try to do as much as I possibly can in that window. Let me multitask, you might think – after all, my mind is up for it. However, by focusing on one thing at a time at this crucial part of my day, I am able to reduce clutter and distractions while also boosting my focus, energy, and success on important tasks.

In the words of Gary Keller and Jay Papasan, the authors of *The One Thing*: "It is not that we have too little time to do all the things we need to do, it is that we feel the need to do too many things in the time we have."

To select what I will work on at this time, I often ask myself "What is the one thing on my to-do list that will have the greatest impact?" The premise is that various activities and tasks have varying levels of impact.

Therefore, plan this time in tune with the importance of each undertaking. As Keller and Papasan say: "Sometimes it's the first thing you do. Sometimes it's the only thing you do. Regardless, doing the most important thing is always the most important thing."

However, the morning might not be the best time for everyone; you might be a night owl, and that is perfectly fine. It really doesn't matter what time of day these principles get done, as long as they are done on a consistent basis.

This isn't just about thinking. It's about dedicating your time wisely and surrounding yourself with what you need in order to keep up your creative output. To some people, this means creating a block of time where you can dedicate your focus. To others, it's more about rescheduling any creatively demanding tasks to the time of the day when you are at your peak performance.

Find Your Best Hours
Sometimes, creativity oozes out of us effortlessly; other times, you find yourself moving from task to task trying to avoid any engagements that may demand us to engage our creative sides. When planning out your routine, it is best to position creative-demanding tasks at the periods of the day when you're at your best.

The mornings work best for me, and you should also strive to pin down your creative times as well. If you're not sure, I will give you some pointers on finding your best hours.

Protect Your Creative Time
It's sadly all too easy to let life encroach into the times you've blocked out for creativity. You need to ring-fence those times and keep them safe. That means saying "no" to conflicting commitments – but it also means trying your best to avoid interruptions and distractions while you're working.

Turn off the phone, close the door, and shut out the world for an hour or two. Make this an appointment with your most creative self. It is the time to reach far and beyond in both imagination and action.

If you have very important tasks to accomplish, this is the best time to do them. By dropping everything else and focusing on key tasks at this creative time, you'll get a lot more done in the long-run.

Finding Your Productivity Peaks
You can find your most productive work times and patterns just by paying closer attention to your habits. The first step to accomplishing this is conducting a self-evaluation about when your energy and focus levels are highest.

'Are you an early bird or a night owl?' If there's a clear answer, then schedule your work hours based on this if possible. Regardless of starting time, always be sure to prioritise your tasks based on importance and/or deadline.

If there's a big, time-sensitive assignment on your to-do list, work on it when you have the most energy. If you are not sure about your creative peaks, keep an informal diary of what you accomplish throughout your workday.

Over several days, say a week, you can identify a pattern which will help you re-structure your workday so that you make the best use of your productivity peaks. You can also ask your colleagues when they observe you to be in peak performance and when you appear lacklustre. You are guaranteed to find your creative time using one of these methods.

Next, determine what holds you back from getting all your work done. Productive people will often say that their secret is excellent time management, but not everyone is naturally good at it.

A recent user survey by time-tracking software Toggl found that, while most people practise some sort of time management (only about 4 percent said they don't), there are numerous obstacles they face in doing so. Among the top answers were:

- Not setting priorities
- Poor planning
- Distractions
- Underestimating the effort a task will take
- Procrastinating
- Multitasking
- Doing things last minute

Keenly evaluate these reasons and make a note of the ones that are hampering your productivity. Once you know what's hindering your tasks, you can then work on replacing those habits with positive ones so as to become more productive.

Summary

Despite our best efforts, and caffeine intake, we are not always at our peak. Everyone undergoes productivity peaks and slumps at different times of their daily routine. To make positive progress in life and business, you must make the best use of your time at peak performance – your creative time.

This will call on you to prioritise your work. Start with tasks bearing the greatest impact and to focus on one task at a time. If you don't automatically know your most creative time, you can use an informal diary to discern your productivity pattern or even ask your colleagues.

After finding your creative time, identify and eliminate all factors that may negate your performance at this time. Incrementally, you will start to see your overall productivity and performance grow over time.

Action Points

Making the best use of your creative time is a crucial step towards attaining success in the property business. Have you identified your creative time? If yes, break down your goals into actionable tasks then allocate them various times of the day depending on importance and impact.

Lastly, identify and eliminate all factors that might lower your productivity during (though not limited to) your most creative time.

CHAPTER 5

The Importance of Consistency, Routines and Repetition

> "Success is neither magical nor mysterious. Success is the natural consequence of consistently applying basic fundamentals."
> — Jim Rohn

You might have heard the saying: If you are persistent, you will get it. If you are consistent, you will keep it. Everyone wants consistency, whether it is in regard to running a business, investing, supervising employees, dieting, exercising or parenting. Consistency develops routines and builds momentum. It forms habits that become almost second nature.

For example, think about one of your goals. It requires consistent effort to push toward that goal. If you are not consistently focused on achieving it, you will likely fall back into old habits or lose interest. Being consistent is the difference between failure and success.

Leadership guru John Maxwell said: "Small disciplines repeated with consistency every day lead to great achievements gained slowly over time."

Developing Consistency

Consistency is a steadfast adherence to the same principles, course, form etc. If you can stick to what you promised to do, long after you have said it, even in a different set of circumstances, people will surely say that there is consistency in your pattern of behaviour.

When customers are seeking your services, they expect good results all the time. If you or a member of your team slips up even with minor transactions, you will lose the trust of these customers. Your consistency is what will build your reputation.

However, as the saying goes, it takes years to build trust but only seconds to destroy it. Therefore, earning a good reputation is not an end in itself, the real work is in maintaining and building upon that good reputation. The property investment business is marred by constant disruptions and when customers come to you, they expect that you can offer them some predictability or assurance. If you can do this, they will be happy and they will return.

As the leader of your property investment business, portraying consistency of attitude and behaviour is not only good for the business at large but more specifically for your team. Your consistency will set a good example for your team. Trust between a team and the boss is built upon consistency.

By earning the trust of your team, you will save a lot of time through reduced conflict, higher productivity, and morale. Even the most dedicated team members will sometimes become demoralised due to unavoidable circumstances in and out of the workplace. However, it is up to you as their leader, to set a standard of enthusiasm and positive attitude in the face of afflictions.

The consistency of thought and action will ultimately make the difference between failure and success of your property investment business. In the long-term, consistency will create a synergy that will radiate across the business: cementing how you relate as an organisation and also how you attend to your customers.

Establishing A Routine
A routine is a sequence of actions regularly followed - otherwise explained as a fixed schedule of events. As a person who loves to travel and do things my

way, I would understand why using the word routine might sound contradictory. You may automatically think of a strict schedule with no free time, no room for fun and spontaneity.

However, from my twenty years of running successful businesses, I can confidently say that designing and adhering to a personal daily routine is the path to productivity, freedom, happiness, and fulfilment of our true potential.

Having a routine provides a sense of structure or a way of organising your life so that you are in control of your life. This order will save you a lot of decision paralysis and procrastination - where you are caught up doing nothing because you don't know what to do. When you wake up, you feel in control, you know what you intend to do which will naturally motivate you to accomplish daily tasks and also build momentum to reach huge long-term milestones.

Your routine will eventually form your habits. This will not only help you eradicate bad habits but also build on the positive habits. Positive ideas and actions will become automatic without necessarily having to plan or think about them.

In this manner, you will always be on top of your business obligations while also saving time for yourself and your family. If you have always wondered about the secret to work-life balance, having a routine that works for you is your best bet.

Understanding The Power Of Repetition

Repetition is the recurrence of an action or event. If you want to learn a new skill, perfect an old one, achieve a goal or change the dynamics of your property business, repetition is the key. The premise is that you are trying to change a paradigm – beliefs, ideas, and habits etched in your subconscious mind. In this regard, repetition erodes past ideas and beliefs and in their place, you install the desired ones. You must note that this is not a product of strong will or memorising new ideas but rather a result of consistent and repetitive exposure to the new ideas.

In the words of motivational speaker, Zig Ziglar: "Repetition is the mother of learning, the father of action, which makes it the architect of accomplishment."

The simplest manifestation of the power of repetition is thinking back to when you were learning to ride a bike. At first, it was impossible to balance yourself for two seconds.

After several falls and bruises, you could ride unassisted for several metres. Eventually, it became part of your life and now, when referring to simple tasks you say "It's as easy as riding a bike". This is the power of repetition. Therefore, identify a skill you want to learn in your property business or otherwise, and relentlessly repeat it through trial and error and soon enough, it will be as easy as riding a bike.

Summary

What did we learn? First, consistency is an important foundation of successful property investors. It will earn you trust among your employees and customers alike. This trust will nurture your reputation which will always speak louder than your words. You build consistency by having a routine. How? A personal routine blends obligations into your life leading to efficiency, productivity and an all-round organised and enjoyable life.

The best and only way to embed a routine in your life is through relentless repetition. This will demand more than will and desire. You have to dedicate time and effort to perfect new ideas, habits, and beliefs. Eventually, positive ideas and actions will become as easy as riding a bike.

Action Points

Model your best self and work towards consistently being your best self. What attitudes do you want to install in your property business, what narrative do you want your customers and your team to take from your business?

Identify the habits that foster this image and relentlessly practise them so that they become your way of life.

CHAPTER 6
Do Less to Achieve More

> "Improved productivity means less human sweat, not more."
> — Henry Ford

I recently came across a blog that posed a very mental question. "Is it too little butter or too much bread?" That got me really worked up and I could not wrap my head around the concept to decide which is which.

But looking at it from another angle, it dawned on me. When was the last time you thought to yourself, I have too much time to complete this project? Or, I have too many resources for this undertaking?

I can guarantee that the answer is a vehement no. There is always never enough time for all that we want to do and even less resources, if any, to further all our goals.

Conventional knowledge tells us to work even harder and when the time is right, things will fall in place, but I beg to differ. Just as busyness does not imply importance, doing more does not guarantee achieving more.

We tend to wear our busyness as a badge of honour such that the more time you are seen taking calls, replying to emails and pitching to clients, the more likely people will perceive you as accomplished, important and successful. Additionally, we often think: the more I can deny myself of pleasures and take on mounting pressure resulting from my job, the better I am at doing my job – a sign of good character. Conventional wisdom urges us to work harder so as to achieve more.

The truth is that busyness is nothing more than cognitive overload and an overloaded brain never inspires performance. As a matter of fact overloading our brain impairs our ability to solve problems, organise, plan, make good judgements, learn new things, remember the second name of our clients, speak fluently, control our emotions etc. And yet scientists will say that we have more computing capability than the most powerful computers, we are not computers by any stretch.

We get tired and bored, unlike computers. Switching between tasks, though refreshing at first, disorientates our minds after a while, and we become more prone to make simple errors. When faced with a very important project, we intuitively try to keep off distracting devices and activities and focus at that one task alone. This is the opposite of busy and sure enough, because we are settled, we worry less about keeping up with time but on successfully completing the single task.

Our society is currently driven by a "more culture". What do I mean? We are constantly seeking a more prestigious job or transaction, more cars, more money, more activities for our kids, more likes on social media and the list never seems to end - we want more of more.

As a society, we are encouraged to think that more is better but is more really more? Taking a step back from this belief, you will find out that what we have is sufficient and that the "more" we are chasing is nothing more than a pie in the sky.

In the medical profession, there is a term they use to describe the perfect medication, MED – Minimum Effective Dose. This is the lowest dose of a pharmaceutical that achieves a clinically significant improvement in health. We ought to find the MED in everything, both in personal life and in business.

This concept is not devoid of contradiction. Most entrepreneurs including myself are addicts of success, we love getting our hands dirty and seeing things materialise. As a matter of fact, leading property business owners such as multi-millionaire real estate entrepreneur, Grant Cordone, constantly advocate that you are either all in or you are all out. Do we conceptualise this to mean that we bury ourselves with work? Of course not. It is about finding our perfect MED.

After I had my surgery, I spent quite some time contemplating my goals. I knew I wanted to make quantum leaps in many areas of my life. Several inspirational books and self-reflections later, I realised that the key is not to work harder or do more but to actively come up with ways to think more, do less and raise my productivity.

Enter my "Miracle Morning" and daily routines. I have stuck to this way of life ever since and I can sincerely attribute most of my recent success to this approach to life and work.

Learn To Prioritise

In *The One Thing*, Gary Keller and Jay Papasan put across this concept in a very clear and concise manner. When we are faced with a swarm of activities, the truth of the matter is not all of these activities carry the same weight and impact. Keller then poses a fundamental question that is a critical part of my morning routine: what is the one thing that I can do now such that by doing it, everything else becomes easier or unnecessary?

By answering this question as I start my day and during my planning sessions, I am able to wrap all my activities into 3 to 7 critical activities that bear the most impact and weight. I then prioritise these activities in order of urgency with the ONE THING being the first activity of the day. I get started with my day with a clear-cut logical plan that at close inspection allows me to do less while achieving more.

We all have endless to-do lists. As a matter of fact, they always seem to be getting longer every time we cross off some of the tasks. The key, as I have learnt, is to be ruthless in making priorities. By extension, this means saying no to time-wasters. In the words of Steve Jobs, "You would think focus means saying yes, but it actually means to say no".

Looking at Steve's business model, it was not just talk. When Jobs returned to Apple after being ungracefully expunged, he ruthlessly cut the line-up of their products from 350 to just 10. Those are a lot of hard and ruthless "No's" for one man to deliver. Looking at the trajectory that Apple then took after this painful but necessary re-evaluation, you quickly realise that it was the best decision he could have made. While saying no to otherwise polite requests may prove difficult, it is necessary and it ought to be done.

According to the Pareto principle, the 80/20 concept, only twenty percent of your brain activity produces 80 percent of your income. To put this into perspective, it means that 80 percent of your activities are time-wasters and just 20 percent are productive. Detect what your 80 percent time-wasters are, say no to them and pay extra attention to the 20 percent that have real impact on your income and goal achievement.

Manage Your Time Creatively

There is one great equaliser among all people and that is time. We all have equal amounts of time at our disposal. According to many, time management is the single most best kept secret of the rich. I beg to add to this with: it is not just time management but also the management of our energy. Dr. Mehmet Oz, a renowned surgeon, is keen to note that the things we do ought to give us zest for life.

Just as we capitalise on finding the optimal return on our investment in business, capitalise on finding the optimal return on your energy. If something is draining your energy and straining your ability to enjoy life, then you are working hard against your own good. Remember that if all was to be taken away from you, your happiness is what would hold you up.

I want to demystify one thing. Productive work does not always have to involve 'doing something' and here is why. I am always amazed by high ranking officials both in business and in governance. Take for example, the people who work for the Queen or the Prime Minister, you will never see them typing, filing, balancing a statement etc.

But without their presence, many things will go astray. These officials spend most of their time thinking, directing and making decisions. Those activities are the highest return to their energy and in that moment, they are at their peak work performance.

What do we take away from that? For one, you do not have to do everything by yourself. Take the time to do more thinking and to empowering others to execute your ideas. This is a better use of your genius. Secondly, doing nothing is not a waste of time.

As a matter of fact, when we appear to be doing nothing, our brains retreat into day dreams and imaginations and this is the peak of our creative insight. This is the time we come up with new ideas, refine old ideas and conceive out-of-the-norm solutions that wipe out competition. Do you know why Steve Jobs called his company Apple? Spending days in an apple farm "doing nothing" is not a waste of time.

Learn To Take Time Off

In the current and emerging economy, efficiency and effectiveness in the workplace is and will be measured by how much knowledge you are contributing rather than the amount of physical labour you put in. In essence, your future lies between your ears and no longer on your hands. It is your ability to think productively, creatively and innovatively that will spur you to make a mark in the market.

Peak cognitive abilities only come about from a well-nurtured brain. Just like a pressure cooker, your mind needs to let off the steam that builds up over time. Give yourself time to relax and de-clutter your mind or else your mind will overflow, cause ailments and will no longer be needed by others. I am not advocating putting work aside and eating life with a big spoon.

On the contrary, I am advocating that you integrate periodic rests into your work routine as a critical part of improving efficiency. Change your work environment from time to time, decide to work on your pitch in the public park, reply to emails by the pool or on the balcony and if you have the means, travel to another city and work from there.

Incorporate relaxing activities such as meditation, exercise time with family and so on into your work routine and you will notice a huge leap in your ability to be creative and objective. While you can always catch up on yesterday's work tomorrow, you can never undo a missed date, a chronic back pain or missed time to talk with your ageing parents.

In the words of James Patterson:

"Imagine life is a game in which you are juggling five balls. The balls are called work, family, health, friends, and integrity. And you're keeping all of them in the air. But one day you finally come to understand that work is a rubber ball. If you drop it, it will bounce back. The other four balls ... are made of glass. If you drop one of these, it will be irrevocably scuffed, nicked, perhaps even shattered."

Summary

Achieving more is not an obvious result of doing more. We attain our peak genius when we leverage our full cognitive abilities on the most important activities. While tasks are unlimited and resources strained, it is important to realise that however important tasks seem to us, they all have varying levels of impact and priority in the grand scheme of our goals. Learn to be ruthless in cutting away time-wasters from your life.

Prioritise important activities by focusing on the one thing that supersedes others in impact and weight. Additionally, you do not have to do everything by yourself. Learn to delegate and focus on areas where you are most effective. Lastly, it is in vain to work hard if your mind is disoriented.

Appreciate the value of taking time off to regroup and nurture your mind. Remember, other than your mind, family and friends are your greatest investments and assets.

Action Points

Have a look at your goals. Focus on your goals. What are the three most important goals for the year, quarter, month, week and today? Decide on who and what is important and cut out the rest.

Learn to say no to people and activities that distract you from your set goals. Above all, busy will never translate to importance, so value your off time.

Go for walks, plan a vacation with your loved ones, change your work environments, exercise, meditate and focus on keeping your cognitive abilities and energy levels at their optimal levels as we discussed in the previous chapter.

CHAPTER 7
The Liberation of Personal Growth

> "Whatever the mind can conceive
> and believe, it can achieve."
> — NAPOLEON HILL

This particular topic is one that is very close to my heart, not that the rest aren't, but I am a fervent believer that for everything else to fall into place, you have to deliberately take actions that facilitate your progress.

This is personal development – a personal commitment to continually seek to acquire new skills and knowledge, sharpen old skills and knowledge and foster an environment that facilitates you to achieve a higher goal. This commitment has allowed me not to relax during my high points and also not to despair during my low points.

When I was diagnosed with cancer, it dawned on me that I had settled into a comfort zone. I wasn't pushing myself and I wasn't growing. I realised that this was a real low point in my life, so to overcome this I decided to set new visions and goals for myself. Etched in this resolution, as I have mentioned, is a morning routine that is inspired by *The Miracle Morning*. I like to begin my day positively which also helps me to accomplish more throughout the day.

As always, I wake up around 5am and I like to wake-up slowly. What does this mean? Basically, it is doing things in a non-rushed, stress-free way. I always do this before I start my work for the day.

Luckily, I work from home, so I am able to do this fairly easily. But if you are finding yourself stressed, or forgetful and not as productive as you could be, I would really advocate waking up 30 - 60 minutes earlier. I'm not saying 5am, but just 30 - 60 minutes before your usual time. I know, it's easier said than done but you will quickly get used to it and the benefits are absolutely amazing.

Imagine just being able to make your coffee, and/or breakfast without being in a rush to get off to work. Sit outside on the balcony or in the garden, and just relax ... wake up slowly, and your day starts off so much better. You will have a less stressed day and get much more done.

When I am in Bangkok, there is a nice park with a small lake, near where I live and in the morning, just after sunrise, I love to walk there and carry out my morning routine. Because it is not too hot at that time of day, the park is abuzz with people running, exercising, groups carrying out tai chi, or just out with their children in the play areas. So it is great to wake up slowly and experience what everyone else is doing.

Generally, I sit down on the grass near the lake, and carry out my morning routine I talked about earlier, which is based on Hal Elrod's *Miracle Morning*.

My zeal for personal growth and development has allowed me to be proactive instead of waiting for things to happen for me. I go out of my way to influence them to happen. While I may not always be able to achieve my desired goal instantly, I become more inspired by the gradual positive changes I make in my life.

Things like installing new habits, having a sense of direction in the face of uncertainty, resilience in times of hardship. I also devote time to make more effort at fulfilling relationships both at work and with my family. The key pillars of my personal development approach are:

- personal goal setting
- learning plan
- meditation
- affirmations and visualisation,
- reading and writing
- exercise
- volunteering and helping others
- mentoring
- mastermind groups

Personal Goal Setting

Whilst I still have some way to go, I have achieved a lot of the things I have set out to accomplish which means that I am satisfied with my business and I'm not considering shifting to a new one. However, most people shift from one business to another or rush everywhere trying to do more but end up achieving very little.

I can argue that the difference between the people who are satisfied with what they are doing and those who have to shift from time to time lies in how each person sets their goals. I am always keen to ensure that I apply the SMART system when setting my goals. By setting SMART goals, I am able to:

- clarify my ideas
- focus my efforts
- use my time and resources productively
- increase my chances of success in business and life

What is the SMART system?

The SMART system consists of the criteria through which I judge my goals before embarking on them. In summary, my goals have to be:

- Specific (significant, simple, sensible)
- Measurable (motivating, meaningful)
- Achievable (attainable, agreed)
- Relevant (realistic, results-based, realistic and resourced)
- Time bound (time limited, time/cost limited, timely, time-based, time-sensitive)

Here are some examples of the smart goals I have set in my property investment business:

- I will raise £1 million in investor finance in the next 12 months
- Offer on 20 new properties that pass our appraisal system
- Options signed on atleast three planning gain projects

Learning Plan

In addition to ensuring that my goals are smart, I try my best to align them with the targets on my learning plan so as to ensure that I have an organised progressive learning trajectory. A learning plan is a structured and supported process through which I reflect upon my own growth, performance and/or achievement through a distribution of topics across various months as the need arises.

My learning plan, therefore, stresses on the areas that I need to improve on due to recent slack and/or areas that are important according to the time of the year and the state of the property market. If there is a trend that is coming up which I feel will affect my business, I make it my agenda to acquire as much knowledge on the same as I can. In this manner, I am not caught off guard by business trends or other pertinent obligations.

As the name suggests, a learning plan helps me to plan for the attainment of short-term and long-term goals. To develop a learning plan, you must identify your goal through the smart system we discussed earlier. Additionally, identify the areas of business and life that you need to work on, or which may be a prerequisite for future endeavours. Then, identify activities that increase the likelihood of success in these endeavours.

You can distribute the various topics across the year as they become relevant. For me, I categorise the topics I feel that I need to learn into four areas: sales, business, property and personal. This allows me to have a wholesome learning experience in all areas.

Download a copy of my learning plan template and other bonus documents here:

http://www.freedomviaproperty.com/downloads

Meditation

Meditation has been shown to have very significant effects on the quality of our minds. By taking time, early in the morning, to just relax and think about nothing or to recite self-reassuring mantras, your brain loses all tensions which effectively relieves stress and increases happiness. It is like unloading all the baggage of the previous day and starting with a clean slate.

That way, you are bound to have more cognitive abilities and awareness throughout the day. The practice has also been shown to slow ageing and boost a healthy lifestyle. I'm sure we all want to remain young and healthy.

Meditation is a big part of the Asian culture and having experienced this culture in the numerous times I have been there encouraged me to include meditation in my morning routine. I prefer to sit on the balcony or in the park and just calm myself down using the 'CALM' app on my phone, which is great for guided meditation. I truly believe meditating regularly has given me an inner peace that has helped me control my stress levels massively.

Affirmations And Visualisations

To understand the importance of affirmations and visualisations, think about this for a minute.

- Your achievements are a result of your actions
- Your actions are a result of your decisions

THE FOUNDATIONS OF A SUCCESSFUL PROPERTY INVESTOR

- Your decisions are a result of your thinking process
- Your thinking process is dependent on the quality of your mind.

Meditation will improve the quality of your mind but that is not all. You have to skew your thinking processes towards positivity and effectively towards what you want to achieve. I believe that you have to see it in your mind, affirm and re-affirm before you can manifest it in real life.

Here are examples of affirmations I have used in the past:

- I have found a number of joint venture partners
- I will build a successful property business that doesn't need me
- I am confident
- I can achieve anything that I want
- I am successful now but I want more
- I am a multi-millionaire

I spend 5 - 10 minutes per day on visualisation, where I visualise 5 - 6 really important things I want to achieve in my life. I try to go into great detail. For example, I want a new Ferrari, so I visualise myself sitting in the car, looking at every aspect of it, including the yellow and black prancing horse logo on the steering wheel, how it makes me feel driving it, etc.

Another visualisation exercise I perform is to see myself with a portfolio of hundreds and hundreds of properties that generate passive income. I see my monthly bank statements showing significant amounts of money. I reflect on the positive feelings that come from this.

After I have finished with visualisation, I then spend 5 minutes or so on affirmations, which I use to instil confidence, break any issues I am having and reaffirm long-term goals.

Incidentally, I will use visualisation and affirmations in a more short-term context as well. So, let's say I have an important meeting to go to, I will use these techniques before the meeting, to relax myself and influence the outcome of the meeting. If I can visualise a positive outcome, it generally happens.

Before I go into a meeting with a land owner for example, I visualise a positive meeting. I have an aim in mind of what I want to achieve and I visualise us both shaking hands on a deal which provides me with what I want.

In the words of T.E Lawrence, "All men dream, but not equally. Those who dream by night in the dusty recesses of their minds, wake in the day to find that it was vanity: but the dreamers of the day are dangerous men, for they may act their dreams with open eyes, to make them possible."

Reading And Writing

In Hal Elrod's book, *The Miracle Morning*, he advocates reading and writing as part of the routine. Generally if I am out and about walking, then I will be listening to a personal development or autobiographical book on Audible.

When I get home I will write in the journaling app I use called "PENZU", although lately my writing time has been taken up writing this book. In addition to amassing knowledge, reading has been shown to stimulate the mind to sharpen our imaginative and analytical skills which allows us to approach challenges tactically. Reading also sharpens our writing skills which in itself has additional benefits of improving our memory and sharpening our analytical skills.

To boost your reading and writing abilities, you can set aside a few minutes of your day where you read a book of your choice then make a summary of what you've read or try to go further on from what the book says. As you can tell so far, what I write in this book has been greatly inspired by the countless motivational and business books I have read or listened to.

Exercise

As long as I can remember, physicians have always insisted that if you want to feel better, have more energy or even add more years to your life, just exercise. This is especially true considering that exercise has been shown to have monumental benefits regardless of age, sex or physical ability.

In addition to combating health conditions and keeping the body fit, a typical gym session stimulates various brain chemicals that leave the body feeling happier and more relaxed. The improved blood flow and the boost in testosterone and adrenaline gets the body pumped up to take on other daily challenges.

People have different exercise routines depending on their schedules; some in the morning, others in the evening or both. For me it is both. In the morning, generally I will do some yoga, or if in Bangkok, I will walk around the park a few times.

This is not my main exercise slot of the day, but my wake-up-slowly one, where I like to dedicate 10 - 20 minutes of exercise as part of my "Miracle Morning" routine. This puts me in the right mental and physical state to approach my daily activities with zeal and ambition.

However, I will also try to have a one-hour more intense exercise slot which is the time I work my muscles and other parts of the body. Alternatively, I will cycle during this period of the day. In addition to helping me maintain a good physical condition, it also allows me to offload baggage from the day and to have a better sleep during the night.

Exercise goes beyond physical fitness. It also teaches us perseverance and how to set, stick to and achieve goals. I would highly recommend you to adopt the two exercise sessions although it is important that you make sure that the routines are In line with your daily schedule. Before you embark on any strenuous exercise routine I recommend that you consult with your doctor first.

If you are finding it hard to squeeze gym sessions into your schedule, just drop an activity or two from your schedule and dedicate that time to exercise. The short-term and long-term benefits are worthwhile.

Volunteering And Helping Others

It is vitally important that you learn to give back your time and resources to society. Not only is it a needful thing for society but also for yourself. My wake-up-slowly routine helps me oil my engines for optimal productivity throughout the day, but this is not to mean that it should all be about you.

Your giving back could be as small as helping someone else wake up slowly, make your partner or spouse breakfast or coffee in bed etc. Getting that early morning smile, or thank you, will release chemicals in your body that will keep you going happily for hours.

Mastermind Groups And Mentoring

A mastermind group is a small group of people who meet regularly online or offline to talk about goals, growth, and success. They also provide support for one another. In addition to having a group of friends that can nurture your dreams, you also have people that can challenge you, collaborate with you and extend your network.

I can also say the same about mentors who can be part of this group or outside. If you want straightforward, unbiased advice, consult a mastermind group or your mentor. They are a crucial component towards your development. You will often find that within your circle of friends and business partners is where the best answers to your challenges lie.

This is because these are people who understand you inside and out. They have seen your journey, and already have opinions on what you are doing even before you ask for them. Additionally, they most likely have gone through the very same challenges you need guidance on.

THE FOUNDATIONS OF A SUCCESSFUL PROPERTY INVESTOR

Whenever I face challenges in my property business, I always seek the input of friends engaging in the same business. This enables me to avoid generic advice that may result from engaging a professional consultant. Finally, the best source of inspiration and positive criticism, other than yourself, is your peers.

Quite often you face specific challenges in property investment. Let's say that you are experienced in one aspect of property investment and want to move into another area where you have no experience. You are unclear about how everything works in this new area.

When I have been in this situation I have reached out to people who do have the experience. Not everyone was prepared to help but some people were. One of the best ways to overcome challenges is to have a good mentor. I have paid experienced mentors before to have a conversation about a challenge and ask for their advice.

I am a firm believer that to live it, you have to first dream it, affirm it and then work on it. This has manifested itself in my life more times than I can remember. For example, for many years I had been travelling back and forth from the UK to SE Asia, in Economy and Premium Economy seating, however I wanted to fly Business Class but I could never really justify the expense.

So, I added this to my visualisation list. I visualised being picked up by limo, checking in at the business class counter, getting fast tracked through the airport, sitting in the lounge, going into the separate door on the plane, lying back in a fully flat seat and being handed a glass of champagne by the flight attendant.

So, after years of flying non-business class, within six months of this being added to my list, I took my first business class flight to Bangkok ... and it was truly an amazing feeling to finally achieve something that I had wanted for such a long time.

In the words of Muhammad Ali, "It's the repetition of affirmations that leads to belief. And once that belief becomes a deep conviction, things begin to happen."

CONCEIVE ... BELIEVE ... ACHIEVE

Summary

Early mornings are very important to me, not only because they are my creative times, but also because they help me shape and influence my day. Based on Hal Elrod's *Miracle Morning*, I have developed a wake-up-slow routine that allows me to engage in positive activities that influence positive outcomes in my day. I am also able to maintain good moods, remain stress-free and be more productive for the rest of the day.

I highly recommend that you select some, if not all, pillars from my morning routine and start practising them. It will surely have a positive impact on your business and your life.

Action Points

What the mind can conceive, the body can achieve. Each morning is a clean slate to rewrite your future. Identify positive activities that can help you gear up for the day full of zeal and positivity.

As with everything related to our thought process, make it your routine, habit and eventually your life. You can pick some of my pillars why not get yourself a copy of *The Miracle Morning* by Hal Elrod?

CHAPTER 8

Do You Need To Learn About Yourself?

> *"No man is free who is not master of himself"*
> — Epictetus

In the famous trial of the Ancient Greece philosopher Socrates, the philosopher famously stated that "the unexamined life is not worth living". In this trial, Socrates was accused of disregarding the gods and for 'corrupting the Athens youths' by encouraging them to challenge accepted beliefs and to critically think for themselves.

Socrates was found guilty and given the liberty to choose his penalty including exile, death or remaining silent. However, Socrates believed that a life in exile or remaining silent was contrary to the core that gave life its meaning.

Socrates firmly believed that the purpose of life was personal and spiritual growth through self-examination using a process that is now known as the Socratic Method. At its core, it is a process of having conversations with others which helps to reveal flawed thinking and blind spots that you are unable to see yourself.

According to Socrates, unless you are free to examine and reflect on your life, you will not grow. Socrates was sentenced to death but is celebrated the world over for his firm and practical belief in self.

CHAPTER 8

As a property investor and business owner myself, I derive great inspiration from that story and I firmly believe that this is a lesson that every aspiring or growing entrepreneur needs to learn.

Which is, that unless you reflect on and examine your life, you will not grow, develop or reach your potential. It is through self-examination that you come face to face with yourself and get to understand your motivations, desires, values, strength, weaknesses and talents. Consequently, it is in addressing these personal attributes and flaws alike that lays the foundation for success in life and in business.

Knowing one's self is part and parcel of the route you have to take to become a successful property investor. As a matter of fact, I have always found it paradoxical – a sort of chicken and egg question. Do entrepreneurs become an entrepreneur because they are searching for more gravitating situations that harnesses their attributes or does the search for self-enrichment and satisfaction in life shape people to become entrepreneurs?

Whichever side you fall on this discussion, it is undeniably clear that success is tied to self and that is only realised by those who ask the right questions about themselves and then proceed to plan in accordance to the insights they acquire. It is only as you examine your life that you are able to identify the changes that you need to make to boost your growth and success in life and in business.

Success Begins With Leading Yourself

The process of growing as a successful property investor is synonymous with personal development. This is the more reason why knowing yourself is the foundation of achieving success in business. You cannot begin to steer a business without having a good idea of who you are as an individual.

You first need to know yourself and what you want to make out of your life. This is the foundation of achieving a strong character, authenticity and purpose.

It is only after understanding who you are, and not what the world thinks you are, that you are ready to lead.

According to Warren Bennis, author of *On Becoming a Leader*: "No one sets out to be a leader. People set out to live their lives, expressing themselves fully. When that expression adds value to the people around them, they become leaders. Therefore, the point is not to think first of becoming a leader but rather to become yourself, to use all of your skills, energies and gifts in making your vision manifest."

Acquiring a deep understanding of who you are as an individual and where you are going provides the context for where and how you can succeed. The quest for success in life and in property investing is therefore first an inner quest to discover oneself and what one cares about.

It is in this process of self-reflection and self-examination that one finds the awareness needed to steer one's life or business towards success.

The Process Of Knowing Yourself – Self Awareness

As we identified earlier, learning about you means having an accurate understanding of your strengths, values, weaknesses, beliefs, desires and motivations. Successful entrepreneurs have mastered this self-knowledge by committing to consistently and continually improve their self-awareness.

Seneca, the Roman philosopher, is quoting the Greek philosopher Epicurus here:

"A consciousness of wrongdoing is the first step to salvation"

This remark of Epicurus' is to me a very good one.

And Seneca goes on to say: "For a person who is not aware that he is doing anything wrong has no desire to be put right.

You have to catch yourself doing wrong before you can reform."

The term self-awareness is defined in the Oxford Dictionary as the conscious knowledge of one's own character and feelings. Self-awareness is based on an honest reflection and assessment of very many attributes: one's personality, strengths, character, weakness, beliefs, values, desires and motives.

To break this down further, let us use the analogy of a mirror. We use a mirror in order to have a detailed insight into our appearance. The reflection you see in the mirror provides you with information that you can then use to adjust your appearance.

As such the mirror, and by extension the reflection it makes, is a catalyst that helps you identify the changes that you need to make. In the same way, self-awareness gives us information about ourselves and what we need to change in that regard. It is a catalyst for personal development, growth and change.

> "Observing yourself is the necessary starting point for any real change."
> — CHALMERS BROTHERS.

I will summarise the process of self-awareness into three pertinent questions:

1. Why is self-awareness important to me?
2. How do I become self-aware?
3. What do I need to be aware of?

Each of the above questions evokes a deep sense of personal self-search that yields personal awareness. We are all different in our own right and it is expected that we will not come to the same answers to the above questions. However, the process is the same and the result is the same even though the routes may differ slightly.

Why Is Self-Awareness Important?

I am yet to come across a superhuman other than on film. We are all human and are limited in one way or the other. It is in taking account of our abilities and appreciating our limitations that we can succeed. The premise is the following:

Starting The Right Business Requires Knowing Yourself

The fact that you are reading this book means that you are either in property investment or are thinking of joining us in this industry. All the same, knowing your strengths and what you enjoy sets a foundation for a business that you can fully commit to.

In this case, you easily deal with business problems that are best suited to your skills and interests and which are less sensitive to your limitations. Too many people make the mistake of getting into property investment because it is lucrative or because their friends have recommended it. For a fact, you cannot be happy or successful working in a business that does not speak to you on a personal intimate level.

One of the strengths that I posses which has really worked for me in property investment is going with my head rather than my heart. I never form an emotional attachment to a property like some people do. It is all about logical thinking and decision making.

Another one of my strengths is attention to detail. This has helped me immensely when I have been appraising properties and performing due diligence.

A third strength is patience. I always stick to a plan and never concern myself with the fact that I have not done a deal in a long time. I never go out and just purchase a property just because I haven't done this for a while. It always has to be the right thing.

To Attract The Right Team, You Need To Know What You Don't Know

Self-awareness is not only a recognition of our strengths but also of our weaknesses and shortcomings. In truth, failure in business is in the most cases a result of blind spots in our foresight and skills.

You, therefore, need to surround yourself with the best people to complement your strengths and fill in your gaps so that together you can see the real opportunities in their entireties, set the right objectives and see them through to success. Many property investors under-perform because of having a team that does not blend with their person.

Building A Successful Property Business Requires Confidence In Self

As the leader of your business and by extension an entrepreneur, you have no one to hide behind. Knowledge of one's self is the key to confidence and confidence yields leadership. It is this leadership that will develop your market, attract potential customers, motivate the team and conquer the challenges that your business will face.

In some cases, challenges might be out of your range and the ability to capitalise on your strengths and accept input from your advisers and team will allow you to be effective. You will give the image of a strong, non-autocratic leader, who is a good listener and who knows how to tackle the many challenges of running a property investment business.

The biggest challenge to a property investor is finding the right properties to invest in. Then comes finding the money to purchase the properties and refurbish them. It can be a challenge dealing with banks and solicitors as well. If you are in the buy to let market then you have the challenge of finding the right tenants.

Being Authentic And Genuine Gets The Best from Others

Your team looks up to you for support and guidance. To gain respect from your team, your team must see that you not only like, but are confident in, who you are.

In the same way, clients and partners outside the business also respond to this vibe and in turn give you the respect and trust that you need to lead the business effectively. Respect and trust are what are needed. It is always painful to continually being something you are not.

Knowing When To Say No Without Guilt

Not every opportunity, however lucrative, is the right one for you. As such, in this modern age where opportunities are readily and easily available, it is important to appreciate your limits. In order to survive and flourish, it is best not to take on tasks which you cannot deliver, or which are not priorities.

If you know yourself well enough, you never have to use the common excuse, 'I have a lot on my plate currently' ever again. You can say no outright with reason and conviction.

These justifications speak to various types of people and may vary from person to person. After developing the conviction on why it is important to know yourself, you then need to adopt channels through which you can learn about yourself.

How To Master Self-Awareness

It is true that the first steps towards success are always inwards. To become a successful entrepreneur in the property industry, you must know how to master who you are and also have the ability to harness your inner power, intuition and instincts.

Knowing yourself with clarity will ultimately lead you to the deals that are right for you and to the ventures that work for you. If you fall short of self-awareness, you will always have a hard time dealing with the counterforce of out-of-control emotions which can pull you down very fast. To master self-awareness, you can do the following.

Become Inwardly Directed

I strongly believe that no one is a repeatable phenomenon in this universe. As such, we all have different capabilities we can bring to the world. To develop these capabilities, you must culture an inward drive or force that will motivate and propel you to work hard at mastering your skills and harnessing your strengths.

This inner sense of direction will push you towards attaining your goals since it gives you a pathway through which you can express your individuality in your business. You have a personal legend to live, and going inwards is the first place to tap into this inspiration.

Learn The Ropes

Property investment aside, in any business that you may venture into, it is incumbent on you to learn the ropes. You ought to know the bottom line mechanics of the business you are venturing into as well as how to stay afloat in adverse conditions.

Some of the bottom line mechanics for a property investment business will include:

- Knowing the numbers
- Calculation of profit margins
- Appraising the true value of a property
- Knowing the demand in an area
- Knowing the average house prices in an area
- Knowing average rental yields in an area
- Accurately calculating refurbishment costs

You need to learn these bottom line mechanics because all the excitement and zeal of venturing into a business can easily be quashed as the inevitable feelings of boredom, fear, impatience and confusion start to set in. To rise above this obstacle, as an entrepreneur, you need to master these emotions and their causes.

From my experience, the best way to learn this is to follow the lead of others and to master how things fall together. By investing yourself in this process, you are going to develop the confidence you need to master your path. The thing is, you have to humble yourself and appreciate that with practice comes fluency.

Master Emotional Control

History has proved that great leaders are also great masters of their emotions. As a leader, you need to know when to evoke your emotions to push for power and the attainment of objectives. But you also need to know when to pull back and let people use their self-drive. The last thing you need is to be overwhelmed by fear or anger when making critical decisions.

Rational thought keeps a person in touch with the overall long-term picture. This enables you to make well-reasoned decisions that are beyond petty emotions.

Exhibit Curiosity

As entrepreneurs, we yearn to move from one level to another. We are always looking to introduce new investment strategies, improve existing services, and so on. This drive emanates from an emotional force of curiosity and desire.

We are curious to see how far we can go, how much we can achieve and how big it can be. This curiosity evokes personal realisations and consequently growth. It is through this drive to do more that we actually realise that it is possible – we do have the potential to reach beyond where we are currently.

You must never be content with where you are or what you have achieved or built. In the words of Steve Jobs: "Always stay foolish always stay hungry".

What You Need To Be Aware Of

Mastering self-awareness calls on you to look inwards and do an honest self-evaluation. The major impediment to self-awareness is trying to be like someone else. You need to ground yourself and know what works for you.

As long as you are seduced by other people's lives and try to be like them, every new idea will appeal to you. Choosing a project indiscriminately is never a good idea. You may often find out that you do not have the necessary answers or the technicalities to exploit the opportunity. This will be all too late because you have gone ahead with the investment.

An example of this in property investment is if you purchase a property at an auction. If you are successful with your bid, as soon as the hammer goes down on the sale you are totally committed and you have exchanged contracts on the property. In most cases you have 28 days to complete on the purchase.

If you have not been to see the property beforehand to check it out or your solicitor has not checked out the legal pack prior to you making your bid, if a problem arises, you could land yourself with a big problem. For example, your solicitor might uncover a covenant on the property preventing you from doing what you want with it. If the discovery is after the bid there is nothing you can do.

No one else has the answers but yourself. Mentors and peers might offer valuable input but you know you best. This might range from major aspects of our lives to the simplest of attributes that differentiate us. These are some of the personal things you need to establish and then include in your journey.

Am I A Night Owl Or An Early Bird?
The rule of thumb here is: work only when it is most natural to you. If you have a family or other commitments, you should find a compromise to lean into. For instance, maybe you cannot work all night till 7 in the morning as you would wish because you have to prepare your kids for school. Well, work till 3 am or 5 am. You can always find a compromise. Again, there are profound benefits to working at your most creative time.

Identify Your Needs
Some people are poor with morning meetings and I am one of those people. This is not a bad attribute in the least – I am not trying to vindicate myself here. I have touched on the fact that I always want to wake up slowly and the

thought of having an early meeting tends to make my sleep antsy. I prefer to start with my wake-up-slowly routine before I can get on with the business of the day – this works for me.

For other people, they cannot sleep without having something scheduled for the morning otherwise the whole day will be slow. They always want to wake up and hit the ground running, attending a meeting or seeing clients. I understand their needs.

What Mitigates The Feeling Of Being Overwhelmed?

It is normal to feel overwhelmed because, despite the best of our efforts, not everything will happen as planned. This is not necessarily a bad thing. As a matter of fact, you may have scheduled just one client meeting for the day but another client comes up and by your best assessment, you cannot pass up on that deal.

This may trigger a feeling of being overwhelmed or losing control. Identify the root of this feeling and either reschedule or make different choices. You can even politely let a client down for the sake of other weighty issues without feeling guilty.

Do You Perform Better In Solitude Or In A Community?

It is difficult to pretend to be someone you are not. Some people find it hard to work in open office setups because they need quiet to keep their rhythm going. Others feed off the buzz of fellow team members.

Instead of trying to fit in, find what works for you and plan your work to fit into your liking. You can opt to work from home, the public library, your balcony etc. Whatever you decide, you will definitely see your productivity go up.

Be Cognisant Of Your Strengths and Leverage Them

This is pretty obvious. The only way you become an expert in anything is by practising. If you are good at back-end operations, lay your focus on that and let someone else take on the part of meeting clients and negotiating. The reverse is true.

Many property investors get stuck trying to be the superhero in their businesses. They want to be involved with everything which is not always possible. Make the best use of your strengths but also acknowledge your weaknesses

Society today keeps us busy and engaged and in this fast-paced rhythm, it is difficult to slow down and reflect.

However, everything else is in vain if you are not self-aware. To build the property investment business you have envisioned, you need to take a step back and learn about yourself.

Summary
The great philosopher, Socrates, up until his death, believed that it is only by thinking for and about the self that one can really grow. The now-famous Socratic method of self-examination advocates that the purpose of life is personal and spiritual.

It is only through self-examination that one gets to examine and come to terms with one's desires, motivations, fears, values, strengths, weaknesses, and talents. This understanding and appreciation is what will lay the foundation for your success. You cannot start to steer a property business if you do not know and understand yourself.

Additionally, self-awareness tells you what you don't know and helps you attract the right team. What's better is that you only need to show curiosity about the self, master emotional control and let the inner drive dictate more of the person you are and are going to be.

The life application of self-awareness allows us to identify our needs and recognise and mitigate feelings of being overwhelmed. It also allows us to be in tune with our strengths and talents so we can leverage them.

Action Steps

Self-awareness can only be evoked by the self, of course. You are your own doctor in this situation. To get in tune with yourself, meditate, yes. Take some time off to improve your moment by moment awareness. Pause and reflect. Personally, I practise this almost every morning by simply appreciating and focusing on my breathing.

At this moment, you can ask yourself what you are trying to achieve, what is working, what might be slowing you down and also what needs to change.

You can also write down your priorities and plans. This is a common method applied by the most successful investor in history, Warren Buffet, when he makes an investment.

You can also seek honest feedback from trusted friends and cordial colleagues at work. We all desire to be self-aware. It is the key to self-congruence. This is a situation where what we say, do and feel are consistent.

CHAPTER 9
The One-Hour Principle For Working On Yourself

"Work on yourself more than you do on your job."
— Jim Rohn

You have everything in this book that you need to make the necessary changes to develop a success mindset that will prepare you for winning with your property investment business. The important thing is that you don't just agree with the things that I say but actually take action and work on your personal development regularly. Each time you spend time working on yourself you will build momentum on the previous time. This leads to exponential growth rather than linear growth which is what you want.

Think about this. If you invested just one hour of your time a week for personal development in a year you would have spent 52 hours. This will have a significant impact on your life and your success. What if you were able to do more? What if you could spend a few minutes each day doing this? Successful entrepreneurs work on their personal development a lot. They know that by doing this they will reach new heights.

In every chapter of this book there is an Action Points section which I encourage you to follow. So after reading each chapter do not move on to the next chapter without completing the Action Points. This will get you into the habit of working on yourself regularly. If you spend a week reading a chapter and working on the action points then that's fine. It is also fine if you read the chapter in a couple of hours and then work on the actions. It is entirely up to you. The important thing is that you spend time regularly improving yourself. The more time you are able to spend the more positive changes you will make faster, leading to improved results.

The One-Hour Principle

The one-hour principle enables you to laser-focus your effort on personal development in a consistent, creative manner, that will not overwhelm you, enable you to break things down into really small chunks, focus on one thing at a time, and produce amazing results in just a matter of months.

TRUTH: If you dedicate just one hour per week to "working on yourself", you will be classed in the very small minority of people that ever do this.

You are responsible for setting goals and thinking about the future. You are also responsible for ensuring that you grow all of the time and keep shifting the boundaries of your comfort zone. When he was president of the United States, Barack Obama still made time to read for an hour each day. The most famous investor in history, Warren Buffet, dedicates 80% of his time to reading and thinking about the future. Bill Gates is one of the world's richest people and he still reads a book every week. He also takes a two-week reading vacation every year. If these people can find the time to do this then you can too. Don't fall into the "I don't have enough time" trap. It may not be easy at first, it wasn't for me, but you must find time to work on yourself.

If you can only spare an hour a week to begin with then that's fine. As you progress and start to see positive change you will want more, and it will be easier for you to increase the time that you invest in yourself. The important thing is that you spend some time on a regular basis. If it is one hour per week to begin with then stick to this for a while.

It is really easy to make a start with this. Treat the Action Points that you follow at the end of every chapter of this book as your regular commitment to personal development. After you have completed the book and all of the actions you can develop a regular success routine. Daily is best, but a few times a week will also produce great results for you.

Don't focus on the fact that you don't have time. If you are really that busy then work out how you can make more time. What about getting up earlier each day than you do now for example? As I have mentioned, I get up early every morning and spend time working on myself. There is nobody around so I can comfortably spend time meditating, visualizing, reading and planning as well as other things. I started with one hour per week and have successfully progressed from there.

How important is it to spend time working on your personal development regularly? I can tell you with absolute certainty that the time I have spent working on myself over the years has been the most important investment I have ever made. Challenging myself and developing a winning mindset has got me where I am today. I will continue to do this as often as possible.

Concentration And Focus

Better concentration and focus make life easier and more productive, and anyone can make it happen.

It's been said that the greatest power of the human mind is its ability to focus on one thing for an extended period of time. If you've ever held a magnifying glass in the sun, you know how scattered sunlight can be focused to start a fire.

So concentrate your brain power into one bright beam and focus it like a laser on whatever you wish to accomplish.

In their excellent book *The One Thing: The Surprisingly Simple Truth Behind Extraordinary Results*, Gary Keller and Jay Papasan talk about how success can be accelerated by focusing on just one thing at a time, so forget about multi-tasking. Focus, focus, focus.

And there is an important focusing question that is mentioned throughout the book:

"What's the ONE Thing you can do such that by doing it everything else will be easier or unnecessary?"

The One Thing is well worth a read.

So, let's get focused, break things down into small chunk and, work just one hour per week improving your mindset. Now start to change your life so that you build the foundations of a successful property investor.

Summary

If you want to be a successful property investment entrepreneur then you need to be prepared to make the mindset changes that will get you there. Failure to do this will bring you poor or mediocre results. All successful entrepreneurs work on themselves. Consistency, as I keep saying, is the key to success.

Time invested on your personal development is the best investment you can make. There will always be new challenges for you to face in the property investment business, and without the right mindset you will find yourself under a lot of pressure and it will be very tempting to quit.

Start by adopting the one-hour principle. Make a commitment to work on yourself at least one hour a week to start with.

Action Points

Use the Action Points in this book as your starting point for working on yourself at least an hour every week. Each time you read a chapter complete the Action Points and continue to do this until you finish reading the book.

Draw inspiration from the book *The One Thing* to decide what to focus on and improve your concentration power. Improving your focus will enable you to get more done and stop being distracted by other things around you.

CHAPTER 10

Why Knowing The Person You Are Is Key To Your Success

> Vision is knowing who you are, where you're going, and what will guide your journey
> — Ken Blanchard

Knowing the person you are is a critical realisation both in your personal and business life. It is the starting point towards our success, and by extension, wealth.

In this case, wealth is not about money but rather our natural path of least resistance where we are following our flow. As a result, whether you are making money or not, you know that it is the right path for you.

You discover your path of least resistance by first identifying who you are in terms of your entrepreneurial profile. I know of some people who spent a large part of their lives doing something they saw others do; only to realise later in life that the only reason they failed was that they didn't know or follow who they really were.

Some people are better at communication but poor at details, others are innovative but not implementers. But how can someone know who they really are? How can we identify our talents?

Many methods of finding the person you are have been invented. Some of these methods come at a fee while others are cheaper or free. Successful people are those that identified their flow and capitalised on it. That is talent; following your path of least resistance, the path that you don't struggle to be. This is your natural strength.

I will present different popular methods so that you can use them to identify who you are and to begin your own journey to excellence.

The DISC Personality Profile

Following the work by psychologist William Moulton Marston in the late 1920's, the DISC personality profile test was first developed by Walter V. Clarke in 1940. It examines how an individual ranks in four areas of behaviour i.e. Dominance, Influence, Steadiness, and Conscientiousness. The method is used by individuals looking to identify and maximise their strengths and organisations for putting together high performance teams.

People with the 'D' profile place emphasis on getting results. They have stellar confidence and have a keen eye for the bottom line. They see the bigger picture, are forceful and can be very blunt towards people. Those with the 'I' profile place an emphasis on persuading and influencing others, like openness and are good at making and maintaining relationships.

They are highly optimistic, show enthusiasm, like to collaborate and dislike being ignored. People with the 'S' profile place their focus on cooperation, sincerity and dependability. They prefer to have a calm, composed way of doing their thing without being rushed and are stellar in supportive actions.

The final profile, 'C' represents people who place their emphasis on quality and accuracy, competence and expertise. They like their independence which allows them to think objectively, and focus on the detail. They naturally fear to be wrong.

You can take the DISC Personality Profile test here

https://www.disctest.co.uk/
https://www.tonyrobbins.com/disc/

Wealth Dynamics by Roger Hamilton

This is by far the most popular method of knowing who you are as an entrepreneur. It states that there are only eight routes to wealth and each of these routes represents an entrepreneurial personality profile. Wealth in this case is not money or possession but our natural flow; doing what you know you should be doing and what feels right to you.

These paths/routes are highlighted by successful people who attained their success by following their natural path.

Wealth dynamics puts forth a new view with eight routes to wealth creation. Wealth, in this case, does not infer money or possessions but rather your natural flow – doing what feels right to you. This method puts forth eight profiles i.e. Creators, Mechanics, Stars, Supporters, Deal Makers, Traders, Accumulators, Lords.

The first group of people are the Creators; these are people who are stimulated by making things out of nothing. They create innovative products. They prefer to delegate all other duties so that they can focus on what they know best: creating.

As a Creator, you add more value when you are free to create. As such, you will prefer to have your head in the clouds. Although Creators are not detail-oriented, they can see the bigger picture and will rely on intuition more than facts. This makes them highly likely to think of new innovative things. The downside is that, although they find it easy to start new things, they lack the patience to see them through or complete them and will have many unfinished projects that they hope to get around to in time.

CHAPTER 10

The Mechanics - who are these people? They come second to Creators, they like polishing what has been created but do not involve themselves in the creation itself. They develop a better system; come up with ideas that make businesses look more appealing and saleable.

They have a talent for finding better ways to do things as well as seeing things to completion – they are perfectionists. As such, a Mechanic will have a tendency to rely on other people the least of the other profile types because they trust in their systems and their ability to do better.

The Mechanics, however, retain people around them by changing the systems and changing people in the process. A perfect example is Henry Ford, the founder of Ford Motors who re-invigorated the already invented automobile to fit the middle class.

The Star profile is often misunderstood. However, they are the easiest to spot as their approach to creating wealth is based on creating a unique brand around themselves. Their personal charm and magnetism are their biggest asset.

How do you know you are a Star? Well, if you naturally radiate inner confidence and have no problem taking the lead or being the centre of attention, you tend to be a Star.

Stars are naturally good at creating brands in and around themselves but may fail in developing their success through teams. They can often be frustrated at others who cannot do what they themselves can. This means they are not good managers. By hiring the right managerial team, Stars build enviable brands with the all-time classic example being Oprah Winfrey.

Successful Supporters have the tendency to create their wealth through leading teams of people in meeting objectives. They are people who are born with enthusiasm and energy. They can easily network and bring people together.

While it may take others months to find the right people, Supporters need just one phone call to get results. They do, however, depend on the Creators, Mechanics and Stars to give them something to start with.

For Supporters, the main concern is who to support rather than what to do. Look at Steve Ballmer - in his whole tenure as a CEO of Microsoft, he was able to build his businesses by creating networks through his energetic and lively personality. As a Supporter, your greatest asset is your market reputation while your weakness lies in lack of focus.

Rupert Murdoch is a classical Deal Maker; he is a perfect example of individuals who know when the time to strike is right. He started with a chain of Australian newspapers and now has control over NewsCorp and 21st Century Fox.

As a Deal Maker, you are personable and great at building relationships which means that you are constantly engaging with people from various fields.

Above all, you have a natural gift of timing which means that you are able to connect the right people to the right deal at the right time and for the right amount. Deal Makers take markets by surprise, making millions at a time.

However, Deal Makers will often fail at consolidating their cash flow and run the risk of losing money as quickly as they make it. They are poor at finer details such as accounting and tax – may I mention Rupert Murdoch again?

The Trader's formula for creating wealth is as complicated. They buy low and sell high. They are extremely good at hunting the best bargains and they naturally will not settle for anything unsatisfactory when they know there is a better one coming.

As such, they are naturally good at timing and will often react to events as they happen by means of their enhanced senses. As a Trader, you will most likely have a day by day action plan rather than a year plan – you are ever in the present moment - and effortlessly in the moment at that.

CHAPTER 10

Introverted Traders will use market data and research to master trades, while extroverts will sense the highs and lows from the eyes of the people they are trading with.

As the trading process will involve a very engaging and meticulous analysis of patterns and trends, a Trader may often seem detached from people. The wealthy Hungarian-American investor George Soros stands out as the all-time great in this profile.

An Accumulator like Warren Buffet is an individual who prefers sticking to the successful system. They find a path, exercise patience, discipline and hard work day-in-day-out until they reach their goals. Their strategy to wealth creation is based on collecting appreciating assets.

As an Accumulator, you are likened to the slow tortoise that wins the race. You have a rare patience and prefer to stick with the system of incremental wealth creation making you the safest of the profiles. You strongly dislike risks, and people will often mistake you for procrastinating as you will demand more data before making a decision.

The Lords are those in control. They prefer operating behind the scenes but generate a lot of cash and are known to create wealth by controlling cash generating assets. They control property portfolios, big businesses and companies but you will rarely see them in any of the company premises.

As a Lord, you do not need to own, you only need to control. What does this mean? Take the example of Rockefeller. He made billions from the oil industry without owning a single well. Or consider Lakshmi Mittal who became a billionaire in the steel industry yet did not own any mines.

Lords are cautious, analytical and very meticulous which may often lead others to describe them as controlling. Your nature is to understand real numbers and simple facts. This allows Lords to thrive in tough economic times which is also boosted by their frugal tendencies – they watch every pound.

You can take the *Wealth Dynamics* test here

https://www.wealthdynamics.com/

Each individual falls within one wealth profile. By carefully evaluating who we are, we can easily identify where we belong and start establishing our wealth from what we are naturally best at. It is also important to note that following the wealth creation tactics of another person will often lead to frustration and failure.

You are unique in your own way and to compete on a level playing field, you must learn to harness the best from your personality and wealth profile. The foundation is identifying your personality profile, and making sure that what you do aligns with this profile.

In and by itself, this is success but it will also make other forms of success effortless when developing and expanding your business.

Summary

Success in business and in life will not depend on what you do but rather mostly on who you are. This is not to mean that some people are more inclined to succeed than others. It means, rather, finding your own unique path of least resistance.

Learning who you are, identifying your personality profile are the foundations of a successful property investor. The DISC personality test by Tony Robbins classifies people into four classes each with unique predominant behaviour and inclinations: Dominance, Influence, Steadiness, and Conscientiousness. The 'D' profile carries people with stellar confidence, concerned about the bottom line and in control.

The 'I' profile carries people good at creating and maintaining relationships. 'S' profile entrepreneurs like to do things in a well-planned and controlled manner. The 'C' profile carries people who like their independence and are keen on detail.

Wealth dynamics puts forth a new view with eight routes to wealth creation. Wealth, in this case, does not infer money or possessions but rather your natural flow – doing what feels right to you.

By harnessing your natural flow and applying it to your property business, you not only position yourself for success but the journey there becomes effortless and joyful.

Action Points

There are countless sites offering free or fee-based personality profile tests. I recommend *Wealth Dynamics* as it has a more extensive look at the concept. Identify your profile then sit in a meeting with yourself. Evaluate what you are doing in your organisation currently.

In some cases, you may be the one and all in your company but remember to move to the next level, you have to settle into your natural flow and delegate other duties to other people according to their profile.

If you already have employees, it is easier. Encourage them to take a personality profile test and using their results, align them with their natural flow.

This is the surest way to ensure that your property company is living up to its fullest potential and positioning itself for effortless astronomical growth.

CHAPTER 11

Your Fascination Language – Get Past The First Nine Seconds

> "Communication works for those who work at it."
> — John Powell

If you had nine seconds to impress a client, investor or potential spouse, what would you say? Well, whereas nine seconds seems like such a short time to really make an impression – it is all we get, as science proves.

A recent study released by the BBC shows that the addictive nature of web browsing can leave you with the attention span of nine seconds – that's the same attention span as a goldfish.

It is a fact that our attention spans have been at a steady decline over the last few decades – largely because of technology – and we are learning to think faster and smaller.

In essence, when you meet someone new whether in a professional or casual setting, you only have nine seconds to leave an impact or else the person will lose interest.

When you think about it, this is a really scary thought – nine seconds can be the difference between you and your spouse, investor, biggest client or biggest contract. If that was not pressure enough – you also have to beat competition in that nine seconds.

You see, it is very rare that you will find yourself operating in a monopoly – in which case you do not have to worry much about impressions. So, unless you are 'THEE', say – one with the biggest budget, best quality or best price – you have a huge task of creating and leaving a lasting impression.

Food for thought – Coca Cola, with the biggest budget, best quality and lowest price has probably the most aggressive and vibrant marketing departments.

That aside, the truth is that connections can't happen in nine seconds, true love can't happen in nine seconds, you cannot launch a product, service or movement in nine seconds. However, introductions can happen and do happen in nine seconds. Introductions are like a door, if you knock on the door 'right' it will open and then you can have the bigger conversation. You get to start the relationship, build a connection, launch a company, brand, product, service or movement.

Until that 'door' is opened, regardless of how brilliant you are at what you do, regardless of your track record, accomplishment and educational background – it does not matter.

It does not matter how good you are if no one knows. It does not matter how incredible your ideas are if nobody knows; it does not matter if you are the most brilliant property investment professional if nobody knows.

We do not live in a vacuum and more importantly, creativity does not operate in a vacuum. We have to share our ideas. People need to know and fall in love with what we are offering before they can engage us - we need to fascinate.

The good news is that you can fascinate, we can all compete in this nine second market. That is if we understand and embrace our natural fascination talents. You see, we are born with this ability to fascinate and sometimes it gets beaten out of us in the course of growing or learning to be creative – but we all have it. It is in us – we have these talents.

From the other end, the brain is hard wired to receive fascination – our brains crave fascination, we want and desire to be fascinated. What's more, there is a part of the brain that if we can figure out how to stimulate it, we can shortcut the process of making decisions.

We can cut the decision making process from say a ten-step process to an instantaneous response received in nine seconds. The apex is that there are seven triggers that one can use to trigger this part of the brain, to fascinate people in nine seconds as put forward by Sally Hogshead.

Sally Hogshead, the renowned advertising guru, having gained respect in the industry as early as in her 20s, has worked with distinguished brands such as MINI Cooper and Coca-Cola and has published two New York Times best sellers regarding the Art and Science of Fascination.

And if that wasn't impressive enough, she is one of the 172 living members of the Speakers Hall of Fame. She has developed a "Fascination Advantage Personality Test" and I highly recommend that you look at it after this chapter to discern your fascination language profile.

These profiles are based on seven specific behavioural motivators, triggers, that upon activation, you earn attention – you fascinate. Sally calls them fascination triggers and they include; Power, Passion, Mystique, Prestige, Alarm, Vice and Trust.

Fascination Triggers
Each of the seven fascination triggers creates a different response and consequently a different reaction. For instance, the passion trigger pulls people close whereas the alarm trigger forces people into action.

At a deeper level, the power fascination trigger allows us to take command of environments and markets just like a policeman or Google respectively. The Passion trigger inspires an irrational attraction to other people – you attract with emotion. The Mystique trigger arouses curiosity. It inspires people to want to know more – to want to fill in the blanks just as with a captivating movie.

Prestige increases respect – it makes people desire your stature, accomplishments and way of life just as with royalty. Alarm on the other hand drives urgency, it forces people to act just like HM Revenue and Customs.

Vice, one of the most misunderstood triggers, is the trigger of creativity. It inspires people to look at an existing idea in a counter intuitive way – it redefines the norm. Lastly is the Trust trigger which builds loyalty. It inspires a connection through consistency and stability.

As humans, we activate all of these triggers every day, whether knowingly or unknowingly, to achieve various goals. Brands also activate these triggers but in a more subtle yet deliberate manner to build connections with customers and potential customers.

With humans, we tend to use all triggers in different situations. However, there is one trigger which you tend to use the most – this is your Primary trigger. The primary trigger comes off naturally when you are being your most persuasive.

Additionally, there is a Secondary trigger which influences how you are being your most persuasive. The combination of these two triggers defines your individualistic fascination language.

Your fascination language profile is therefore a combination of two triggers. A person like Rupert Murdoch uses the Power and Prestige triggers – this combination is known as the Perfectionistic Powerhouse.

The late Steve Jobs used Power and Vice – a common combination for entrepreneurs known as the Change Agent. Entrepreneur Seth Godin uses a combination of Prestige and Vice known as the Taste Maker – he sets standards.

The last example is my favourite and is that of Richard Branson. Branson uses a combination of Power and Passion known as the Intuitive Visionary. It is a very likable profile, easy to engage and get along with, but we also respect them and their craft.

My personal triggers are Mystique and Prestige and my archetype is the Royal Guard which means elegant, astute and reserved.

Stand Out Or Don't Bother

In the current highly competitive and distractive market, it's not the job of your customer to find you or define what makes you better – is it not even the job of your consultants. Define your unique fascination language.

As I have consistently stated, to be successful, you do not have to change who you are. Instead, become aware of who you are and use it to your advantage. Knowing your fascination language will help you create better relationships, grow your property business and become more valuable to your clients and prospective clients.

Summary

It is a fact of science that our attention span is diminishing. As of now, you only have nine seconds to make a big enough impression on a person to earn more engagement, or else the person will lose interest and walk away.

Remember that it does not matter how good you are at what you do if no one knows. As such, it is critical that you put your best foot forward when opening the door, to the bigger conversations, in the forming of potential relationships, new clients, new business partners etc.

Whereas it is impossible to build a connection in nine seconds, it is possible to introduce yourself and make a positive, lasting impression in those nine seconds. It is possible to fascinate – and as a matter of fact, it is human nature to desire to be fascinated. You just have to tap in to your natural in-born fascination language.

This unique individualistic language is what pulls people to you – it is what fascinates people about you. This language has two of the seven available fascination triggers i.e. the Primary trigger and the Secondary trigger. The Primary trigger manifests *when* you are being your most fascinating while the Secondary trigger determines *how* you are being your most fascinating.

The combination thereof is what will make people want to listen to you – it is what will keep people around, bring you more deals and investors or even a spouse. The key, therefore, lies in identifying your natural fascination language.

Action Points

First and foremost, look up the "Fascination Advantage Test" by Sally Hogshead to determine your fascination profile. With your result, you must then capitalise on this advantage to be the most valuable you.

Her website can be found here – https://www.howtofascinate.com/

It is your responsibility to get your message heard by the world and the fascination profile informs you what works best for you. As such, what are you waiting for, get out there and make the most impact with your nine seconds.

CHAPTER 12

How To Set Goals That Will Inspire You

> "A goal should scare you a little and excite you a lot."
> — Joe Vitale

There is only one way to achieve your goals and that's by taking action over and over again. We all have wants and desires, we have things we want to accomplish. Whether compacted into goals or just vague aspirations, we all want better things and for things to be better – fact of life.

Another fact of life is that we are always busy, I am busy, you are busy, we are always busy. However, with all the time we spend 'working' we do not always attain our desires and wants. Sometimes, we even do not attempt to achieve what we want, we just wish, wish and wish some more. We know how that ends since nothing comes on a silver platter and if wishes were horses, beggars would ride.

I am a huge advocate for setting goals that help you create and live the life you want. I have seen what setting inspiring goals can do to one's life. It is important that I tell you from the outset that I do not believe there really is a perfect or best way to set or word your goals. As a matter of fact, just having a goal is in itself very powerful – it gives you a sense of direction, a sense of purpose.

However, I've often found that for myself and even the people close to me that if I set a goal that does not inspire me, I am less likely to have the motivation, the fire or the zeal to take action towards making it come to pass.

CHAPTER 12

This is true even when the goal is something that I really want – if it doesn't inspire me, I will gently and subconsciously push it aside while continuing to be 'busy' without any real progress or growth.

As the saying goes:

It is not enough to be busy, the question is, what are you busy with?

If you really want to be and to feel productive and successful, learn to work on the issues that matter to you the most. Having goals is not enough, the question you should ask yourself is, why do these goals matter to me?

If you can find a concrete reason/s, you are on the right path. But this is not always an easy question for everybody to answer. Sometimes and for most people, we just know that we want to do things but we cannot really pin down that which we want to do or even why we want to do it – we just want things to be better.

Therefore, let us take a step back and recap on how we conceptualise actionable goals – goals that rejuvenate our zeal for life and inspire positive action.

Setting personal goals is something that took me a while to master and integrate into my life. I have touched on this in the book but I will repeat that the SMART goal settings are the foundation of all my goals and I believe it's the same for all successful businessmen and women in the property industry and also other trades.

When you set your mind on Specific, Measurable, Achievable, Realistic and Time Targeted ideas, you CAN change your life. I note the word 'CAN' because it denotes potential.

With goals alone, you are like a fully serviced and tuned power generator that is yet to be switched on – you are beaming with potential but unfortunately with no impact in the real world.

This is why I truly believe that we need to feel inspired by the goals that we set. It is the only way that can trigger action and consequently lead to productivity and success. The premise is that, once we are inspired by our goals, we are empowered to act and move towards achieving them.

The truth is that no one sets goals without the intention of achieving them – but only few people take action to see their goals through and people cite different reasons or excuses I should say, for not taking action on their goals.

> "He that is good for making excuses is seldom good for anything else."
> — BENJAMIN FRANKLIN

Goals Vs Problems

First off, I must acknowledge that not everyone is motivated by goals. If you are one of those people, that's okay, it's completely natural. As a matter of fact, there are many people who are not motivated by goals but they do not realise this and so they keep wondering why they never achieve them.

On the other hand, there are people who can set SMART goals that jolt them into action and keep them focused until they achieve them. If you do not fall into that group, no need to worry. Let us look at it differently – let's thinks of goals not as goals but rather as problems that need solutions.

I realise that sounds a bit off but it's just a matter of switching your mindset so that you turn your goals into challenges that you need to rise up to or problems that you need to solve.

Here is an example of buying a car. Let's take it that you are not motivated by the thought of owning a good car – which is possible. Now think of solving the problem of conveniently and comfortably getting from point A to B in a car that befits your desired stature.

While the prospect of owning a better car might not empower you, stepping up to the challenge or addressing the problem of comfortably moving to the office, to the job site or even to meet clients will surely motivate you to act. Therefore, whether you are motivated by goals or by challenges and problems, use whichever inspires you the most.

Decide WHAT Is Really Important To You

This is the first step and it answers the question on WHAT you really want. And if you don't know what you really want, just ask yourself, is there something I need or want to show up in my life?

This will help you unload what is predominant in your mind – what is more meaningful to you at that time. What is meaningful to you can range from career goals, financial goals, investment goals, business goals, health goals, relationship goals or any desire that you feel is right for you.

The ability to pin point the goal or challenge that you really want to achieve inspires clarity of purpose. It inspires you be certain, clear, and to believe that you will achieve that goal or address that challenge. You can feel it in your gut.

> "If you want to live a happy life, align it
> to a goal, not to people or things"
> — Albert Einstein

Uncover WHY Your Goal Is Important To YOU

After setting our goals, it is common for most people to be excited, raring to go and ready to take action. Fast forward a couple of days or weeks later, the initial zeal dissipates and you start giving up on the goal and before you know it, you are setting other goals.

How do you break this trend? Well, write down your goals. This is a practice that I have held onto for several years and continue to do this daily. Every morning I read through my Goal Worksheets as part of my wake-up-slowly routine to remind myself of what I am trying to achieve.

Alternatively, you can use notepad applications provided on mobile devices but for me, I find writing down my goals using a pen and paper much more powerful.

The act of writing down your goals opens up your emotions and connects you to these goals. This emotional connection helps you answer the question why – why the goals are important to you. You then begin to uncover the underlying reason why you want to achieve the specific goal and consequently discover why it is important to take action immediately.

> "If you spend too much time thinking about a thing, you'll never get it done"
> — Bruce Lee

Answering the question why, not only motivates us to take action immediately but also helps us to fine-tune our goals. Let's say for example that your goal is to expand your property business within the coming year. So, why do you want to expand? Why is expanding important to you?

After asking these questions through your thought process, you will finally come up with a more specific goal. Say, I want to expand to xxx market so as to better serve my clients and bring in more revenue. This clarity demystifies vague aspirations and triggers immediate sequential actions that lead to the achievement of the parent agenda.

This resolve on purpose is also informed by being clear on how you want to feel. In her book, *The Desire Map*, Danielle Laporte draws very precise parallels between how we feel vis-à-vis our desires and the resultant success thereafter. In one of the most memorable quotes that inspires me most from the book Danielle says:

"Knowing how you actually want to feel in life is the most potent form of clarity that you can have."

If you are having a problem deriving an emotional connection to your goals, just think back at how you want to feel.

All through my business and personal life, I have noticed that getting clear on how I want to feel enables me to evaluate my goals. If I am facing a couple of conflicting goals or even when facing a tough decision, I work this backwards into "what would make me feel the way I want to feel?"

In effect, this is reverse goal setting which is very instrumental in setting a foundation where you have a deep understanding and emotional connection with whichever goals you want to see through.

Let Your Goals Challenge You

The primary reason why people set goals is to achieve something that they do not have or to move from one stage to the next. As such, we must be willing to challenge ourselves beyond our comfort zones.

A ship is perfectly safe while at the dock, but that is not what it's built for.

It is very easy to fall into the trap of setting goals that are too easy or which are outrightly achievable. Although we set goals so that we can achieve them, it is pointless if the goal does not stretch our abilities and inspire us to be, at the very least, better versions of ourselves.

On the other hand, it is more pointless to set a goal that is too ambitious; then it becomes a burden rather than an inspiration – know the balance. You can easily find this balance by being honest with yourself – you know yourself best.

Ask yourself: does this goal honestly feel challenging to me?

Have A Desired End Result In Mind

This is in tandem to having a means through which you can measure your goal. Creating and holding onto a desired end result helps you to keep on track and most importantly, it helps you to know when you have achieved the goal.

We can create a measure in our minds that tracks our progress on the goal and also informs us when we have achieved the goal. Being clear on the desired end result makes it so much easier to break down the goal into actionable steps that you can get onto immediately.

It also helps you to stay on track – if an activity does not favour or facilitate the achievement of the desired end result, you simply drop it. You have a point of reference, a light at the end of the tunnel, something worth working towards.

However, not all goals are measurable and this is normal and okay. What is important is to keep in mind what the goal means to you and also how you will know that you have achieved the said goal. This may be in the form of a new feeling, the ability to do something you couldn't do before or any other means relevant to your goal.

It is important to have a logical conclusion to your goals as this will derive a sense of accomplishment and inspire you to set new, more challenging goals and have the confidence that you can see them through.

Working without a clear end result can quickly degenerate into frustration while knowing that you have something in mind that you need to prove, do or accomplish derives motivation and indomitable strength to jump out of bed every morning and chase your goals.

Summary

The only way to attain your goals is to maintain a high level of motivation to attain them from start to finish. However, it is very easy to get caught up in the practise of getting busy without really making real progress on our goals.

While setting goals is a powerful step towards success, only positive, deliberate actions ensure that you attain the desired success. Otherwise, you are just a powerful super-car continually revving at the starting line. The key lies in setting SMART goals that trigger action. If such goals do not inspire you, you can change your mindset to view goals as challenges that you need to overcome.

If goals do inspire you, you then need to set goals that inspire such action. Herein, the key is to identify what is important to you and also why it is important to you. If you know what you want and why you want it, it does not take much to figure out why you need to keep striving for it.

As a precaution, avoid setting goals that are too simple – those that do not trigger you to be better at something or goals that are over ambitious – those that end up frustrating you.

Lastly, it is important that you have a means of measuring the goal so you know when you are done. If the goal is not particularly measurable, set milestones that inform you of your progress. Having goals that have no means of tracking often end up in frustrations. As such, identify the what and why in your goals and watch your goals steer you to success.

Action Steps

1. Create a list of everything that you want to achieve, have, or desire from all aspects of your life. Make a list of at least 50 – 100 things, so for example, you might want to get married, lose some weight, buy a new property, own a Ferrari etc. Write down everything you can think of from your personal life, business life, family life, what you want to learn, who you want to help etc.
2. Next to each item, write down if they can be realistically achieved within 1 year, 5 years or 10 years.
3. Choose five to seven items that really inspire you, that can be realistically achieved in the next year. Choose from different categories,

so don't just have all monetary or business goals, it is best to have a mix.
4. Complete my Goals Worksheet, so that you have it clear in your mind and to make sure it is written down.
5. Next set weekly appointments in your diary to review your progress. At the meeting you will think about what you have achieved towards that goal, write it down and find a next step.

    So, on the back of the Goals Worksheet, write down the date, and what you have achieved that week. Also, in the "Next Steps Area", you must write down at least one thing that must be achieved/done to get you closer to your end goal. Also, cross off any "Next Steps" that were achieved last week.
6. Add your next step onto your to-do list or project management program and make sure to allocate some time that week to working on what you want to achieve.
7. When the goal is achieved, mark through the whole sheet using a highlighter pen, COMPLETED and file it away in a specific folder. Celebrate the success, by treating yourself to something. This process is very important as it gives you a massive dopamine hit, and will make you feel fantastic.
8. Now choose another one year goal, and start working towards that, with the same method.

I have a Goals Worksheet that I use all of the time. I have had a lot of success using this over the years.

Download your FREE Goals Worksheet and other bonus documents here;

http://www.freedomviaproperty.com/downloads

CHAPTER 13
The Importance Of Knowing What You Need And What You Want

> "When you know what you want, and you want it bad enough, you'll find a way to get it."
> — JIM ROHN

This is a more practical chapter but no less important. In fact it is probably the most important chapter in the book. Knowing where you are currently, knowing what you want for the future and what your level of financial freedom is are vital foundations for any successful property investor.

Without fear of contradiction, allow me to start this chapter by stating that: Work is About Money. I know it sounds wrong but this is a silent truth that we have all come to accept.

Work only elevates from not being about money only when one can consistently earn sufficient income that can support your lifestyle of choice. Point to note: the definition of sufficient income varies across people, based on lifestyle preferences.

When you finally crack this form of utopia, work stops being about money and becomes about making a difference, contribution, feeling important, gaining success, making friends and leaving a legacy. Before then, let's talk about maximising your income earning potential through your property business.

The amount of money that you want to make, and what you do make, during your lifetime is dependent on your business choices. In essence, you cannot earn a million pounds a year if you stick to a business that pays you £40,000 per year.

The situation is easier for those who are employed as they have a certain degree of assurance with regards to their earnings. As a property entrepreneur, money is the salary you pay yourself from your business. This amount is solely dependent on the kind of business and the welfare of the business.

Contrary to popular notion, I strongly believe that money is neither the root of all evil nor the panacea for all the worries in life. However, it allows us to support ourselves and our families, do philanthropic work, travel, purchase luxuries, pursue hobbies and interests and even allows us to retire if one pleases.

In simpler terms, money is what money can do. As such, maximising your earnings is not only okay but also fundamental to the quality of life. It is therefore only rational that we endeavour in activities that bring in more money. However, if you are not already financially free the starting point is knowing how much you NEED to make to be comfortable.

How Much Money Do You Need To Make?

This is not a question that most property investors really ask. To most people, the primary goal is to maintain positive cash flows in the business and driving business growth.

However, that is not enough and I will tell you why. If you are looking to get more from your business than just the ability to get by, you need to be certain that your investments can sustain you and your family even during your retirement or maybe sickness. To arrive at the right figure, you need to spend time analysing your current situation. An easy way to do this is to brainstorm every expense that you have and put it in a spreadsheet. I have an example for you later on in this book.

The common things that you will need to have in the list include; Living expenses – rent, utilities, food; Debt – student loans, business loans, car payments; Insurance - business risk, car, life, health; Leisure Money – shopping, travel, miscellaneous. Again, the list of expenses will differ from person to person based on lifestyle choices.

This is also a good time to conduct a critical analysis of your monthly expenses and even look for ways to manage your expenses better.

The next thing you want to do is to set aside some money for savings. Yes! It is very important that you learn to treat savings as a responsibility rather than a favour that you give to yourself when you are in the mood. When it comes to savings, I recommend having three types of savings – preferably in different accounts to avoid losing track.

Emergency savings. Professional financial advisers recommend maintaining 6 – 12 months' salary in this account. Also, it should be a liquid account preferably with a level of interest. This is to caution you in case of personal emergencies.

Retirement. As you are reading this book you probably own, or are thinking of owning, property. Properties are great retirement funds and acquiring assets is a good retirement strategy. It is never too early to start thinking about retirement. Even though entrepreneurs never really retire, you need to save up for your later days. When you own income-generating properties you may not need to save additional money for your retirement as they will provide the income that you need. To make it easier, start off with an annual figure and then work out how much you need to save monthly or even weekly if your business allows.

Additional savings. The above two savings funds are critical to a financially secure life. Most people make the mistake of taking off money from the above two pools and using it on luxuries such as buying a new car, boat, vacation etc. This is not only wrong but dangerous. Realising these individualistic goals will call on you to dedicate supplementary long and short-term savings accounts depending on the particular goal.

To finally come up with a total figure, you need to add your savings requirements to your expenses. This figure will give you the basic minimum amount of money that you need to earn. To get the annual figure, just multiply the amount by twelve – this is your annual earning expectation.

Here is an example for you.

	Monthly	Annually
Living Expenses		
Mortgage / Rent	£1,000	£12,000
Gas / Electricity	£50	£600
Water and Sewage	£45	£540
Rates / Council Tax	£60	£720
Groceries	£400	£4,800
Other	£250	£3,000
Communication Expenses		
Telephone	£75	£900
Broadband	£30	£360
Debt		
Student Loan	£55	£660
Car Loan	£115	£1,380
Insurance		
Life Insurance	£80	£960
Car Insurance	£110	£1,320
Home Insurance	£50	£600
Fun Money		
Travel	£200	£2,400
Shopping / Clothing	£250	£3,000
Entertainment / Subs	£200	£2,400
Savings		
Emergency Savings	£100	£1,200
Retirement	£200	£2,400
Additional Savings	£30	£360
Pre-Tax Total	£3,300	£39,600
20% Tax	£660	£7,920
Totals	**£3,960**	**£47,520**

According to the above calculation, this particular property investor needs to make

£3,960 monthly and £47,520 annually. A good exercise is to work out the hourly rate you need to cover these expenses.

What is your hourly rate?
Calculation Example:

Income needed: £47,520pa
Hours worked per week: 50
No of weeks worked per year: 48
No of hours worked per year: 2400
Hourly rate is: £19.80

After you have established the money that you ought to be making in an hour, it is time to identify the income streams that will ensure that you maintain this rate.

How To Meet Your Targeted Hourly Rate
Very important... stay focussed!

Income diversification is old advice that has been known to increase business earnings. However, the success of this tactic relies on making sure that the cost of diversification does not negate your profits.

As a rule of thumb, diversification could increase your income but I believe staying focussed on income generating tasks (IGT) is highly critical. Narrow down and focus on those activities that bring in more revenue at the least cost.

In our example earlier in the book our property investor needed an hourly rate of £19.80. If they only work at tasks that generate £19.80 or more then they will reach their financial target.

For every hour that they spend on tasks that are not generating this, they are costing themselves money, which will ultimately lead to not being able to save enough or pay their bills.

This concept is a vital one to grasp:

IGT = pay bills and save

Non IGT = no money

So a good property business and good life in general, is centred on making good decisions. These decisions include where to invest, which ideas to implement and what to prioritise.

The fundamental question to maintaining your desired hourly rate is to decide which business to work on, which properties or strategies to focus on, which services and products to offer as well as what target markets to go after and what IGTs you will work on. This is called the goal of validation where one puts intensive thought around where to spend your time and effort with the effects of earning the best results.

For me this is one of the key foundations to build if you want to be a successful property investor. This process answers very important questions with regards to the position of your property business, its prospects and also its structuring in the face of the prevailing business environment. It creates a pause and reflect moment. This kind of decision making – deciding which IGTs to pursue does not always come naturally to all people. However, a helpful tool to ease this decision making is inversion. Inversion has the effect of making a good decision by not making a bad decision.

In simpler terms it means maintaining a healthy income stream by not rushing into decisions. After all, it is easier to avoid stupidity than to achieve brilliance. This evaluation will allow you to narrow all your activities into the most profitable both in life and by revenue.

If an activity falls out of your favour – it does not support your income expectations, you may choose to completely do away with it or outsource it to a professional. The implication is that you are freed up to focus on those parts of your business that can and will bring you maximum revenue given your time and lifestyle.

The Importance Of Knowing What You Want

You now have the tools to work out what you need in order to pay your bills and save, but you need to go a step further and figure out what you really want. The £47,530 per year figure in the example takes care of our property investor's survival and savings requirements, but you will want to earn much more than that going forward so that you can have all of the things that you dream about.

You need to set some life goals. Think about what financial freedom means to you and the amount of money that you want in your bank account. Be specific here in terms of the amount you want and the time frame. You have a much greater chance of achieving the goal if it is more specific.

Don't worry at this stage how you will achieve the goals that you set. Set aside some quiet time and brainstorm what you want. Think about the material things that you desire such as a better house to live in, the car that you truly desire, the things that you want in your home, the designer clothes that you want to wear and so on.

Brainstorm what you really want during your most creative time periods and let your imagination run wild here. Write everything down and then you can look back over your list of goals and assess them using the SMART criteria discussed earlier in the book:

- Specific (significant, simple, sensible)
- Measurable (motivating, meaningful)
- Achievable (attainable, agreed)
- Relevant (realistic, results-based, realistic and resourced)
- Time bound (time limited, time/cost limited, timely, time-based, time-sensitive)

Once you have created your goals you will want to refer to them often. Always carry them around with you and look at them every day. You will need to develop a detailed plan to achieve each goal and then break these down into IGTs for regular activities.

Most people do not know what they really want from life. This includes a number of business owners. It is absolutely critical that you set aside some quality time to determine what you want. If you fail to do this then you will just drift along with no real purpose. You may end up making a good living, but there are easier ways to do this. Set the bar high and live and die by your goals.

Summary

Money is what money can do and what money does is give you the life that you and your family hope for. Although ideally work should really be about personal fulfilment, it must first be able to provide you a life of comfort.

To achieve the income that assures you of this life, you need to evaluate your annual and monthly income. Totalling the monthly expenses including savings and then multiplying by twelve, you can then come up with your hourly rate that provides enough money to cover your expenses and savings. To maintain this life, you then need to identify and focus on the activities that maintain this earning, income generating tasks. The best way to identify these activities is validation with the assistance of inversion.

On identifying your core income-driving activities, you need to focus on them and outsource the rest or even drop them all together. This will free you up to make the best of your time and help you actualise your maximum income potential.

Determining the income you require to cover your expenses and savings is just the first step. You need to set aside some of your creative time to establish your short and long term financial goals. If you just use your property business to cover expenses and savings it is like having a job.

Brainstorm what you really want in your life. How much money do you want to see in your bank account? What material things do you desire? Write these in a list and then use the SMART process to create a set of goals that will drive you. It is critically important that you determine what you really want.

Action points

To maintain the life that you desire, you need to have a clear understanding of your monthly and annual money needs. To gain this understanding, prepare a spread sheet detailing your various expenses and savings. Considering the number of hours that you work every day, week, month and annually, you can then work out your hourly rate that maintains your lifestyle.

Use validation to identify activities that support you to meet this rate and then outsource or drop the other activities. Focus on the activities that support your earning expectations and you will become the creator of your destiny.

Set aside some creative time to identify your life and financial goals. Create goals using the SMART process and write them down. Use your goals to drive you forward in your property investment business.

CHAPTER 14
Pulling It All Together And What To Do Next

> "The journey of a thousand miles begins with one step."
> — Lao Tzu

This is the final chapter of the book but it is the start of a new beginning for you. If you have been diligently completing the actions at the end of each chapter then I commend you. If you haven't then I urge you to do this and I have something that will help you focus and work your way through the actions step by step. It is my Workbook which I will talk about at the end of this chapter.

"Knowledge is power" is a quote by Sir Francis Bacon dating back to 1597. Sometimes you will see this quote written as "information is power" but it all amounts to the same thing. Although this is a legendary quote I believe that there is an important element missing. I believe that the quote should be – "information is power only if you use it". You may be wondering why this is important to you.

Don't just read – take action!
Anybody can read a book like this from beginning to end and then not act on the information that they have learned. We have all done this. I have read some very inspiring books in the past and then failed to follow through on

the new knowledge that I acquired. I stopped doing this a while ago and now I always take action when I read something inspirational.

If you just read this book and then take no action nothing will change for you. I did not write this book with that intention. I want you to follow through on what you have read and become the best property investor that you can be. So in this chapter I will remind you of the important elements of each chapter that you have read and what you need to do next.

Chapter One was all about you achieving success your way and not blindly following others.

Key Point: You can achieve success your way

You have a unique voice and personality and you need to create a strategic plan for your property investment business that reflects this.

It is always good to have an experienced mentor because they can provide excellent advice to you. But you do not want to follow what they tell you to the letter. They have their own unique personality and you do too. So take a look at their advice and then think about what you can do differently. Think about your strengths and what works for you. Make your strategic plan around this and use the plan to motivate and guide you to property investment success.

Chapter Two was how success starts with Taking a Leap of Faith

Key Point: Life starts at the end of your comfort zone.

Most people do not achieve what they really want from life due to fear. They get comfortable and rationalise that this is the best they are going to get. You must tackle this fear head on and take a leap of faith every time you are confronted with an opportunity that you are not entirely comfortable with. You need to overcome the anxiety of stepping into the unknown.

Your leap of faith needs to be built on the foundation that with an unwavering commitment and your best endeavours you can achieve anything and be successful. All successful entrepreneurs have this faith. If you fail (and you will sometimes) then you need to learn from this failure. Do not allow the fear of failure itself stop you from achieving your dreams.

All accomplishments and failures in your life should be viewed as milestones on your journey to success. When you were a toddler you had the tenacity and determination to learn how to walk. Keep being tenacious and determined and you will be an unstoppable force in your property investment business and your life in general.

Chapter Three looked at the mindset and success principles of professional property investors.

Key Point: You need the right mindset to succeed with property investment.

You need a big WHY to succeed in property investment. You will have your own reasons for getting involved and you need to be clear on what they are and use them to drive you forward. This will enable you to get through the tough times that you will inevitably experience.

Having a clear and compelling WHY will help you to develop a clear roadmap. You also need to pay attention to the success guiding principles that will help you to succeed as a property investor. There is no need for you to try and reinvent the wheel so don't put yourself under this pressure. Just look to add value to existing systems and processes that have stood the test of time.

Accept that failure is part of your success journey in property investment no matter if you are just starting out or experienced in the industry. Be persistent at all times even when the markets are against you. Quitting is not an option.

Always remain positive even through the toughest times. Positivity will bring success. Get started right now if you are new to property investment. You need to take the plunge because you will never be successful with just good intentions.

Chapter Four focussed on finding and protecting your creative time

Key Point: Find and use your creative time wisely.

We all have a specific time every day when we perform at our peak. This is your "creative time" and you need to identify it and use it to your advantage. My creative time is 6am but yours may be later in the morning or even in the afternoon / evening.

During your creative time you need to prioritise your tasks moving forward. Start with the task that has the greatest impact and always focus on one task at a time. Some people already know when their creative time is but if you don't then you can start keeping an informal diary for your productivity patterns. You can also ask someone that knows you well when your best time is.

Once you know your creative time treat this as a very precious commodity every day. Identify any factors that can negate your performance during this time and eliminate them. By using your creative time every day you will see your productivity and performance grow over time.

Chapter Five stressed the importance of consistency, routines and repetition

Key Point: Being consistent is the difference between failure and success.

All successful property investors are consistent. When you are consistent you build trust and respect. Your reputation is very important and will speak louder than words ever can. Establish a routine to develop consistency. When you have a good routine you become more efficient and productive and you will be better organised and lead a more enjoyable life.

You need to use repetition to your advantage. Repeating a successful routine will bring you the best results. You need to be totally committed here and dedicate the time and effort required to perfect new ideas, habits and beliefs. Once you have mastered this it will be very easy for you to generate positive ideas and take action.

Chapter Six urged you to do less to achieve more

Key Point: Doing more does not guarantee achieving more.

Leverage your full cognitive abilities on the most important tasks. Take a critical look at the tasks that you have in front of you. Are they all really critical for your success? You need to be ruthless and cut out those tasks that will waste time and offer very little, if anything, to get you going forward.

Get into the habit of prioritising your activities and focus on those that have the most impact and importance. Remember that you do not have to do everything yourself. Learn to delegate or outsource and focus on areas where you are most effective. You need to have a clear mind as no amount of hard work will move you forward if you have a disorientated mind.

Take time off to regroup and nurture your mind. Never forget that other than your mind, your family and friends are your greatest investments and assets.

Chapter Seven examined the liberation of personal growth

Key Point: Make a commitment to personal development to relax through the high points and avoid despair during the low points.

Start the day off right. Take a look at my wake-up-slow routine and use some of the pillars from this that suit you and start implementing them. Treat each day as a clean slate where you will rewrite your future. Identify positive activities that will assist you for a day full of passion and positivity.

Chapter Eight asked: do you need to learn about yourself?

Key Point: Unless you reflect on and examine your life you will not grow, develop or reach your potential.

When you go through the process of self-examination you will be able to come to terms with your desires, motivations, fears, values, strengths, weaknesses and talents. This is the foundation for your success as a property investor. You have to know and understand yourself for future success.

When you are self-aware you will learn what you don't know and what skills and talents you require on your team. Be curious about yourself and learn to master emotional control. If you do this then your inner drive will dictate more of the person you are and are going to be.

Be committed to self-awareness for life to enable you to identify your needs and recognise and mitigate feelings of being overwhelmed. You will be in tune with your strengths and talents so that you can leverage them.

Chapter Nine outlines the one-hour principle for working on yourself

Key Point: Work on yourself regularly for extraordinary results.

If you truly want to succeed with your property investment business then you need to work on yourself regularly. All successful entrepreneurs work on themselves regularly and you need to do the same to make the mindset changes required to succeed.

There is no better use of your time than investing in your own personal development. In the property investment business you will always face new challenges and you need the right mindset to deal with these. If you are not mentally tough enough you may be tempted to quit when the pressure is really on.

So make a commitment to work on your personal development at least one hour a week to begin with. You can then increase the amount of time that you spend working on yourself. With this kind of consistent approach you will get results that will inspire you and drive you to success.

Chapter Ten showed why knowing the person you are is key to your success

Key Point: Knowing the person you are is the starting point towards success and wealth.

Your success as a property investor depends on who you are. It will enable you to find your unique path of least resistance. You will be able to leverage all of your natural attributes and talents so that your success is effortless.

When you learn who you are and identify your personality profile you are laying the foundations of a successful property investor. As I have mentioned, there are a number of personality or profile tests that you can take.

The DISC personality test classifies people into four classes that have unique dominant behaviour and inclinations. To recap: these are Dominance, Influence, Steadiness and Conscientiousness. The 'D' profile carries people with stellar confidence, concerned about the bottom line and in control. The 'I' profile carries people good at creating and maintaining relationships. The 'S' profile carries people who like things planned out and controlled. The 'C' profile carries people who like independence and are keen on detail.

With Roger Hamilton's *Wealth Dynamics* there are eight routes to wealth creation. Wealth here is all about your natural flow and not about money or possessions. It is about doing what feels right for you. There eight profiles are Creators, Mechanics, Stars, Supporters, Deal Makers, Traders, Accumulators and Lords. When you harness your natural flow you will position yourself for success in your property business and the journey will be effortless and joyful.

Chapter Eleven encouraged you to develop your fascination language – get past the first nine seconds

Key Point: Use Sally Hogshead's strategy of fascination language to open the right doors.

Because our attention spans are diminishing you only have nine seconds to make a big enough impression for further engagement otherwise the other person will walk away. It doesn't matter how good a property investor you are, if you don't put your best foot forward you will not open the right doors.

You need to use those first nine seconds to make a positive and lasting impression. It is possible to fascinate and to do this you need to tap into your natural in-born fascination language. This is your unique language that pulls people to you so they are fascinated by you.

Your fascination language has two of the seven available fascination triggers known as the primary and secondary triggers. The primary trigger manifests *when* you are being your most fascinating while the secondary trigger determines *how* you are being your most fascinating.

This combination will make people want to listen to you and it will keep them around. This will bring you more deals and investors, or even a spouse. You must identify your natural fascination language.

Chapter Twelve was about setting goals that will inspire your life

Key Point: Set goals that help you to create and live the life you want.

The key to achieving your goals is to maintain a high level of motivation to achieve them from start to finish. Be aware that life is going to get in the way and it is all too easy to become "busy" with mundane things that do not move you towards achieving your goals.

Setting goals is a positive step to success but the only way that you will achieve your goals is through deliberate action. Without this action you will just be spinning your wheels and going nowhere. Always set goals using the SMART process outlined in this book, which will trigger action. If you need additional inspiration then view your goals as challenges that you need to overcome.

For really inspiring goals that will compel you to take action you need to identify what is important to you and why this is important. Knowing what you want and why you want it will drive you forward. Avoid goals that are too simplistic or over ambitious. A goal should always trigger you to be better at something but not frustrate you because they are too easy or unachievable.

You must have a way of measuring your goals so you know where you are and when they are complete. Sometimes a goal is not easy to measure so set milestones so that you know what progress you are making. Goals that are not measurable will be frustrating for you.

Chapter Thirteen encouraged you to know what you need and what you want.

Key Point: Knowing where you are now, what you want for the future and what your level of financial freedom is are vital foundations for any successful property investor.

Money will give you the life that you and your family hope for. Your work must first provide you a life of comfort. So to be comfortable you need to calculate your monthly and annual income. As I have advised, add up your monthly expenses and include your desired savings. You need to establish your hourly rate which will cover both of these things.

You need to focus on the activities that maintain this earning by developing income- generating tasks. The best way to identify these activities is validation with the assistance of inversion. Once you have identified these activities focus on them and outsource or even drop other tasks. You need to free up your time to achieve your maximum income potential.

Determining the income you require to cover your expenses and savings is just the first step. You need to set aside some of your creative time to establish your short and long term financial goals. If you just use your property business to cover only expenses and savings it will feel like having a job, not owning your own business.

Brainstorm what you really want in your life. How much money do you want to see in your bank account? What material things do you desire? Write these in a list and then use the SMART process to create a set of goals that will drive you. It is critically important that you determine what you really want.

Now it is time for Action – Use your FREE Foundations Workbook

I have created a Workbook for you which is specifically designed to guide you through the actions that will lay the foundations for you to become a successful property investor.

Even if you have worked through the actions as you have read each chapter, it will be beneficial to you to go through the Workbook and revisit these actions. A lot of the actions are not "one off" exercises but commitments to changing your mindset over the longer term, so that you can achieve success in property investment on a consistent basis.

So, access your Workbook right now and start working through the actions. If something doesn't make sense to you then re-read the chapter that it relates to. I want you to adopt the right mindset for property investment success and the Workbook will guide you every step of the way.

Download your FREE Foundations Workbook and other bonus documents here:

http://www.freedomviaproperty.com/downloads

Conclusion

It has been an honour to write this book for you. Writing the book was very challenging at times because I wanted to ensure that I included everything that I did to shape my mindset to become a successful property investor. I hope you have gained a lot from the book and will find the Foundations Workbook useful.

I wish you every success on your property investment journey. I would love to hear from you if this book has helped you to achieve your property investment goals. Your feedback means a lot to me and I would love to hear your story. I would also love to learn from you as well, so if you have any ideas or suggestions that would be fantastic.

I have now started a blog about how people can achieve the freedom that they desire through property investment. You can find this blog at http://freedomviaproperty.com/ and the aim of it is to help other property investors gain life and financial freedom. I will be posting all kinds of valuable content on the blog regularly so please check it out and leave me your comments. If you want to contribute content to the blog then please let me know.

So now it is over to you. You have everything that you need in this book to create the foundations of a successful property investor. Use your Workbook to guide you through the process of transforming your mindset so that you are primed for success. There are many challenges to face with property investment and you need to be mentally tough. So make a commitment to work on yourself regularly so that you can overcome any obstacles. If you have any questions at all please let me know.

Finally I want to pay a personal tribute to my best friends and mentors, my Mum and Dad. They played a major role in inspiring me to write this book and have given me unconditional love and support throughout my life and ventures. Thank you so much Mum and Dad, I love you both with all my heart.

Take action today and everyday so that you can become the successful property investor that you want to be. Thank you for reading this book and I wish you every success.

Take care
Harvey Raybould
harvey@freedomviaproperty.com

P.S. Please don't forget to send me your stories and any questions that you may have. Thank you.

Printed in Poland
by Amazon Fulfillment
Poland Sp. z o.o., Wrocław